LIVERPOOL ALEHOUSES:
Including The Wirral

Michael Anderson

Published by Sigma Leisure - an imprint of
Sigma Press, 1 South Oak Lane, Wilmslow, Cheshire SK9 6AR, England.

British Library Cataloguing in Publication Data
A CIP record for this book is available from the British Library.

ISBN: 1-85058-418-4

Typesetting and Design by: Sigma Press, Wilmslow, Cheshire.

Cover design : Martin Mills

Printed by: Manchester Free Press

Acknowledgements:
Mona, for her patience and great help
My mother and father, for their suggestions and support
Lee, for his enthusiastic assistance
Billy 'The Beard' Stapleton, for his friendliness and experience
Duncan McCann, for helpful reminiscence
And to all the landlords and landladies, barmen and barwomen and to all the characters that make the Liverpool alehouse the colourful institution that it is today, my thanks and admiration.

Preface

Considering that Liverpool was once said to have had 'a pub on every corner', making the selections for "Liverpool Alehouses" did not prove particularly difficult. Although quite a few of these corners no longer exist, this great city still offers hundreds of pubs worthy of attention, by virtue of fine architecture, or perhaps an interesting peculiarity, or simply because of some anecdote connecting the pub with a Liverpool gone by.

This book takes a look at alehouses in Liverpool and the Wirral, and discovers some interesting facts: Did you know that Lord Nelson was said to have visited Liverpool and stayed at Rigby's on Dale Street? Or that an American president drank at the Grapes on Mathew Street?

If you are visiting the area for the first time, this book will help you to find out more about Liverpool. Maybe you have lived here all your life, and want to know some of the stories behind your local. Or perhaps you are a student at one of the universities – if so, this book will help you discover where to go to sample the nightlife in this colourful city. Whatever your background, this guide to pubs in Liverpool and on the Wirral aims be an interesting and practical record of a tradition in this area.

The pubs are treated critically, with an eye towards the architecture and atmosphere of the establishments, before moving on to a general discussion of their history. Clear street maps appear at the start of each main section of the book so that every pub can be located with ease. There is also a detailed index which enables you to find not only the pubs, but also the beers that are served and even the street names so that you can find a pub that is convenient for wherever you may be.

Hopefully, this book will present you with an idea of the richness of pub life in Liverpool over the years, and how it has survived and prospered to the present day.

Michael Anderson

Contents

Introduction

*"When you have lost your inns, drown your empty selves, for you
will have lost the last of England."*
Hilaire Belloc

There is probably no other city in Great Britain where the
alehouse is more keenly appreciated or where it occupies a
more important role in the community than in Liverpool.
Evidence in favour of this statement takes many forms. For
example, there are seventy pubs in the city centre alone,
although twenty-two were destroyed during the German blitz
on Liverpool, and many others have been demolished to make
way for redevelopment. Also, the high levels of expertise displayed in the construction and decoration of many of the pubs
in Liverpool, more particularly the exuberant gin palaces like
the Vines and the Philharmonic, show the distinguished standing such establishments have enjoyed in the city over the years.
Some of the more imposing houses were designed primarily as
"prestige houses" or showhouses for the controlling breweries,
who can advertise their products and overtly display their
affluence in such awe-inspiring surroundings. On another
level, alehouses of such architectural importance stand in
memoriam to a time when Liverpool was a busy and wealthy
world port.

Liverpool can boast of so many examples of fine architecture
associated with a city in the prime of its life. The city has two
cathedrals, the Anglican version being the second largest of its
denomination in the world. The Roman Catholic cathedral is
itself very well-known, perhaps more for the contrast it offers
to the austere tradition of the Anglican cathedral than for any

1

laudable features it may itself possess. In a way, the alehouses that abound in the centre of Liverpool are just as important to the life of many Liverpudlians as these impressive places of worship. Both can offer a sort of sanctuary, both connect the people of Liverpool with their history and traditions, and to the average scouser both are equally ritualistic.

Life in Liverpool

Liverpool has always had a strong identity and there is a collective pride in the achievements of the city over the years. A more obvious example is the Beatles and the way the so-called Mersey-beat, and Liverpool life, was brought into a sharper focus by the exploits of the "four lads who shook the world". Their achievements must never be under-rated considering simply the number of tourists who visit the area in search of a piece of the Beatles' story.

Football has always enjoyed a high profile in the city, and with the amicable rivalry that exists between the two great clubs it has almost achieved a religious status, especially considering the fervour of support for both Liverpool and Everton football clubs. During the 1980s, both clubs achieved such high levels of success in domestic and European competitions, that football was the preoccupation of this city almost to the exclusion of everywhere else. The Derby games, despite what some outsiders may believe, are by far the most hotly contested and supported of all local Derbies. Although the city has suffered the tragedies of Heysel and Hillsborough, and as a direct result has seen the end of the famous Kop End at Liverpool and Gwladys Street at Everton, one can be sure that football will continue to dominate the hearts, and the conversations of Liverpudlians for as long as the city stands.

Visitors these days can enjoy the splendid museums and galleries that Liverpool can offer, and more recent developments such as the Albert Dock complex. But for a more rounded view of Liverpool and its idiosyncratic inhabitants, one must venture into that most special and venerated of places, the local pub. Here, you can discover the lively banter, the excellent beers, and the generally warm and friendly atmosphere that Liverpool is famous for. It is only here, where all aspects of life in Liverpool come together and where all types of people gather, that you can claim to have seen Liverpool.

Alehouses in Liverpool and the Wirral

"I regard the pub as a valuable institution"
Sir A.P. Herbert . . . election address, 1935

The Liverpool Alehouse can be as awe-inspiring as the Vines or the Philharmonic, or homely and familiar like the Roscoe Head or the Grapes; or it can offer a direct connection with important figures from the past, as with Ye Cracke and Rigby's. It can take on many forms but taken together, alehouses make up a distinct character of Liverpool that is as refreshing as it is traditional.

The Wirral peninsula offers many pubs in possession of a much different character. Here are fine "country inns", the rural hostelries that for centuries have provided the traveller with welcome repose. Some of them are very old, like the Fox and Hounds in Heswall and the Wheatsheaf in Raby. Others have been renovated quite recently like the Irby Mill, but which still set an example to all breweries of how one can refurbish the interior of a pub without destroying its character.

A Word About the Ale

"Good ale is meat, drink and cloth"
Anon.

Since this book is predominantly about pubs rather than beer, entries are chosen on the merits of architectural interest and historical significance. The ales served in each establishment are printed above the main text of an entry, so that readers may decide for themselves about that most contentious of issues, the real ale versus the pasteurised, fizzed and filtered beer that bears little resemblance to the real stuff. If I have made my own opinion clear on the matter, it was quite deliberate. When one orders a pint of bitter, one should be served with exactly that, a fresh original pint that has not been tampered with or "pre-conditioned" in any way. Some of the pubs in this guide serve real ales, others do not. Fashions change, and landlords of dubious ability come and go, but it appears that the real ale is becoming more popular these days, as people appreciate the vast difference in quality between beers.

Until 1990, Liverpool enjoyed the quality ales produced by the Higsons brewery under Whitbread. After its closure, Liverpool had for a time to make do with imported Higsons produced in Yorkshire, otherwise one had only Tetley Walker of Warrington to rely on. Fortunately, the brewery was bought by a small company who named it after its founder of 1848, as the Cains brewery. Up to now, they have produced three ales of some note, namely Cains Bitter, Cains Formidable Ale (F.A.) and Cains Dark Mild. Cains Bitter went on to win the first prize in the ordinary bitter category of CAMRA's 1991 Champion Brewer of Britain competition, a fillip that was to ensure both the future production of the ale and the success of the brewery.

Many other ales can be sampled in Liverpool, with Marston's Pedigree a particular favourite. Such variety can only be good for the drinker, especially since now many houses offer a guest beer as a temporary alternative to the normal selection. With so many fine ales in production in this country, it is good that one is able to appreciate many of them in one's own local. In conclusion, one would do well to remember the Czech proverb on the subject of good ale that says, "A fine beer may be judged with only one sip, but it is better to be thoroughly sure".

How to Use this Book

The book is divided into three main sections: pubs in the centre of Liverpool, pubs around the centre of Liverpool, and pubs on the Wirral. Within each section, the entries are arranged alphabetically so that they can be located with the minimum effort. There are maps before the Liverpool and Wirral sections and these, with the index, will help in locating the pubs.

Opening Times

Opening hours are as accurate as possible. However, it must be remembered that these times can always change, and if one is making a journey to visit a particular pub, it would be advisable to check. 'Sunday hours' means from 12pm – 3pm and 7pm – 10.30pm. Remember that pubs can open earlier to sell food.

Other Important Details

Information about pub entertainment and catering details is given before the write-up, stating whether a pub has a jukebox or fruit machines and so on. Such details are usually a good indication of the kind of pub on offer, so if one is looking for a quiet drink one should avoid somewhere with a jukebox and live music.

This book is meant to direct you to some of the decent alehouses in Merseyside. It is hardly a comprehensive list, merely a personal selection based on my experiences. The information is historical, or purely anecdotal taken from the stories passed around some places. More likely there are some half truths in these tales, but then the best stories are usually based on these. In addition to everything else, these pubs are to be enjoyed.

"For on this my heart is set:
When the hour is nigh me,
Let me in the tavern die,
With a tankard by me,
While the angels looking down
Joyously sing o'er me,
Deus sit propitius
Huic potatori."
Anon (12th century).

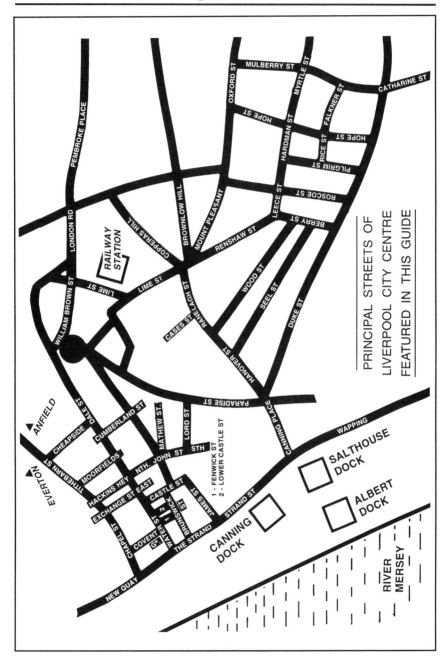

PRINCIPAL STREETS OF
LIVERPOOL CITY CENTRE
FEATURED IN THIS GUIDE

Liverpool City Centre

The Beehive

7 Paradise Street

Opening times: Monday – Saturday, 11am – 11pm; Closed Sunday.
Ales include: Walker's beers.
Bar Snacks/Meals: Yes
Range: Extensive
Live Music: No
Jukebox: Yes
Fruit Machines: Yes
Function Room: No

The Beehive in Paradise Street is a popular pub with city-centre shoppers in search of refreshment, being so close to the main precinct. It is a long, thin pub that feels surprisingly large once inside considering the small front that it shows outside. At one time in its history, it is believed to have been the venue for Chinese theatre, but nowadays it is simply a convenient place to recuperate after the trials of a day spent working or shopping.

Inside the Beehive, the bar stretches along the wall to the right of the entrance, while tall bookshelves line the walls to the left; all around the stained wood and etched mirrors give rise to rather comfortable and genial surroundings. Set into one of the bookshelves, there is an interesting mosaic made entirely from shells, and despite the lingering impression of recent revamping and the introduction of some diner-style seating, the Beehive remains a decent city centre watering hole.

Before the First World War, the Beehive was a Walker's Grill, and there are photographs around the bar showing how the house looked before 1914. Then, the bar was partitioned by wooden screens into separate cubicles, offering the patron an element of privacy while eating. Legs of cooked meat, sliced to make sandwiches, used to stand on the side of the bar, according to a present-day octogenarian patron.

The Beehive is clean and smart but it can be quite noisy,

due to the ubiquitous jukebox. It does get lively, particularly towards the evening, but it is still a pleasant place to rest, and to indulge in the rejuvenating liquors.

Cains

23 North John Street

Opening times: Monday – Thursday, 11am – 11pm;
Friday & Saturday, 11am – 1am; Closed Sunday.
Ales include: Cains, Flowers, Tetley
Bar Snacks/Meals: Yes
Range: Extensive
Live Music: No
Jukebox: Yes
Fruit Machines: Yes
Function Room: No

Cains in North John Street is an unusual pub, occupying the basement of a large office building. In Victorian times it was called the Beaconsfield Café. It was a regular port of call for articled clerks and insurance clerks when luncheon vouchers were given to the employees of large companies as a benefit. It was later called the Beaconsfield Pub, until becoming Cains about ten years ago.

The outside of the pub is rather hidden, being a basement bar, but it is quite stylish, with large globe lights and hanging baskets complementing the exterior. Steps lead down from the street into the bar, and it is soon apparent that Cains has been furnished in the style of a gentlemen's club. Comfortable leather chairs are placed in groups around the bar, which in total occupies quite a large area. Ornate chandeliers hang around the room, with moulded patterns set into the ceiling round them. It is a comfortable place to eat a working lunch, evidenced by the fact that it is a popular drinking den for business men. It is, however, possible to enjoy a quiet pint, with lots of corners offering a little privacy.

The bar itself is quite ornate, and houses an original etched mirror bearing the name 'Jamaica', of unknown significance. The extended licensed hours on Friday and Saturday evenings suggest that it is also a popular weekend nightspot. Although at times music can be played perhaps a bit too loudly, this is a relaxed, urbane setting for a drink that offers an easy escape from the bustle of the business quarter.

The Central

31 Ranelagh Street

Opening times: Monday – Saturday, 11am – 11pm & Sunday hours.
Ales include: Walker's Bitter and Best
Bar Snacks/Meals: Yes
Range: Extensive
Live Music: No
Jukebox: Yes
Fruit Machines: Yes
Function Room: No

The Central in Ranelagh Street was originally a private residence. It was first used as a public house in 1863 when it was called 'The Albion', and nicknamed the 'Sporting House', for reasons unknown. In 1888 the premises were converted into a residential hotel and the name was changed to 'The Central Commercial Hotel'.

The interior decoration of the Central is quite remarkable. Cut glass mirrors on all sides dominate the scene, and the pub is renowned for these. The whole impression is of a glazed palatial interior inspired by the extravagance of nineteenth century affluent Liverpool. There is also a spectacular porcelain cupola just through the door, which is divided into separate panels by gilded borders, each panel bearing painted vines. In the centre of this is a stately chandelier, a jewel amid such splendour. The bar is of an open-plan design, with several different levels where one can drink. The actual bar stretches around the wall to the right of the door.

Any amount of description cannot adequately account for the interior; it must really be seen to be appreciated. Apparently, no efforts were spared in its construction, and it is unlikely that a pub on this scale will ever be built again. It would cost millions.

The Central is another example of the outstanding level of craftsmanship displayed in the architecture and ornate décor of alehouses in Liverpool. It is a testament to the comparative wealth of a city that was once the greatest port in the world, and it is a tribute to the expertise that was available in Liverpool round about this time. A truly noble house!

Coopers

13 Cases Street

Opening times: 11am – 11pm except Sundays.
Ales include: Coopers' Bitter, Tetley, Tetley Mild
Bar Snacks/Meals: Yes
Range: Limited
Live Music: No
Jukebox: Yes
Fruit Machines: Yes
Function Room: No

Coopers in Cases Street is an enticing-looking alehouse from the outside; it appears to be an authentic old house of Liverpool. In the days before Clayton Square, Cases Street used to boast many houses like this one, but these days just the Globe and Coopers survive. It is a thin, tall building and while not as attractive as the Globe, it does sit well on the street.

Inside, the pub is deeper than it looks from outside. The floorboards are bare, and in combination with the etched mirrors, the general feel of the interior is that of a traditional working man's alehouse. The pub is split roughly down the middle so that there is an area at the front by the bar with tables around the floor, and some snug areas at the back of the pub, offering some privacy to the casual drinker. While not lavishly decorated, one feels as though here is a homely, cosy alehouse with a strong local clientele.

Coopers used to be called 'The Sefton', but was renamed presumably after an Ada Cooper who became the licensee on 16 January 1925 and remained so until 1943. This information is displayed on a wooden board fixed to the wall by the snug area and is most probably offered as the explanation of how the pub became known as 'Cooper's'. This is at odds, however, with the pub sign hanging over the door which shows a couple of craftsmen at work making a barrel – perhaps the name was taken too literally!

A feature of this pub is the bitter named after the house. Coopers' Bitter is brewed by Tetley for the pub, and apparently it is a common occurrence for an alehouse in Liverpool to have a brew named after it. It seems a good way of inducing brand loyalty at the very least!

Coopers is a satisfying and refreshing alehouse, that gives us an idea of how the houses around Cases Street would have looked before the untimely intervention of the shopping precinct.

The Cornmarket Hotel
Old Ropery, Fenwick Street

Opening times: Monday – Saturday, 11am – 11pm & Sunday hours.
Ales include: Courage Directors, Theakstons Best, Websters Bitter and a guest
Bar Snacks/Meals: Yes
Range: Average
Live Music: No
Jukebox: Yes
Fruit Machines: Yes
Function Room: Yes

The Cornmarket off Fenwick Street takes its name from the old corn exchange that used to exist around this area. While not as old as the Slaughterhouse, which was where many dealers in grain that frequented the area would meet, the Cornmarket is the last surviving evidence of the extensive business that was conducted in this old commercial district of the city centre.

Inside the Cornmarket, it is surprising how large it is, considering the rather small, undistinguished front that it displays outside. The bar is straight ahead of the entrance and is long, stretching right through to the area at the rear. The décor is really quite tasteful, especially the area to the left of the entrance where the emphasis is on comfort. Here, one can sit by a wonderful ornate carved fireplace. The carvings are extensive, covering the whole of the wall to the left, the dark wood producing a very austere and noble effect. The carvings appear to be of mythical sea-creatures, perhaps reminiscent of The Tempest, and are a reflection of the craftsmanship prevalent in Liverpool from the time when huge liners were luxuriously fitted out with the highest level of expertise available. This area of the pub is completed with sumptuous chesterfields and attractive standing lamps positioned in a way reminiscent of a comfortable gentlemen's club.

It is a pity that the rest of the pub does not match this corner in terms of the lavishness of decoration. A television and a

16

pinball machine detract from what would otherwise be a very grand interior. It is worthwhile finding this alehouse, hidden as it is down a back street; it is very a pleasant, stylish house, let down unfortunately by the tack of modern breweries.

The Crown Hotel

43 Lime Street

Opening times: Monday – Saturday, 11am – 11pm & Sunday hours.
Ales include: Walkers Best, Bitter and Mild
Bar Snacks/Meals: Yes
Range: Extensive
Live Music: No
Jukebox: Yes
Fruit Machines: Yes
Function Room: Yes

The Crown Hotel in Lime Street near the station, was built in 1905 and has one of the richest 'Art Nouveau' exteriors of any building in Liverpool. It consists of a brick superstructure with moulded plaster friezes and gilded letters on a polished granite bas, with shallow box windows to the first and second floors. The architect is unknown, but whoever it was spared no efforts in the lavishness of the exterior detail, or the flamboyance of the décor.

Inside the Crown, there are two different areas to the pub. First, there is the main bar area, simply a large open-plan room around the bar with many tables and chairs. Second, there is an impressive back room. This room is too large to be a snug, and it is remarkably well-decorated, with a panelled ceiling displaying moulded figurines and gilded edges. There is a large fireplace in this room with a copper guard and an etched mirror above. The main bar area has perhaps the most extravagant ceiling of any alehouse in Liverpool. It is a spectacular design, with moulded details all over. Throughout the bar area, there is a good and extensive use of mahogany in combination with copper panels.

Overall, the Crown Hotel is a very stylish house, possibly one of the better known of the alehouses in the centre of Liverpool because of its extravagant exterior. It is popular with shoppers at the weekend, and is normally fairly busy at any time due to its nearness to the station. It is a unique alehouse, with a distinctive character and plan.

Dr. Duncan's

77, Seel Street

Opening times: Monday – Saturday, 11am – 11pm & Sunday hours.
Ales include: Tetley
Bar Snacks/Meals: No
Live Music: Yes
Jukebox: Yes
Fruit Machines: Yes
Function Room: No

Dr. Duncan's in Seel Street is a peculiar place that has a very old feel about it. Although the exterior is really a bit shabby, there is an interesting notice outside explaining just how the alehouse came to be named.

William Henry Duncan was appointed by the Liverpool council to be the medical officer of health for the borough of Liverpool on the 11 January 1848. At a salary of £700 per annum, Dr. Duncan was expected "to give up all private practice and to devote the whole of his time and attention to the duties of the said office". He assisted in enforcing the Sanitary Act in the city of Liverpool, and his work led to the removal of the conditions in the city under which epidemics could flourish. This was very important considering that in 1849 a cholera epidemic swept through Liverpool because of poor sanitation.

Dr. Duncan was quite a man. So what of his pub? For someone who was so interested in cleanliness, it is ironic that a pub named after him could be so run-down. The interior, though, is quite curious. The walls are of a half-timbered design, and in combination with the copper-topped tables and the old furniture, they produce a most unusual décor. There are different areas all around the old-fashioned bar, with a pool table to the rear. A tiny stage to the left of the door accommodates the infrequent virtuoso performances. All around there are old pictures of Liverpool including one of the distinguished doctor himself, which produces a peculiar feeling of time at a standstill. Perhaps this is Dr. Duncan's presence about the place?

Dr. Duncan's is hardly a model alehouse, but it is worth sampling for its uniqueness. Perhaps with a more rigorous enforcement of the Sanitary Act, it could be quite a pleasant pub.

The Eagle Hotel

81, Paradise Street

Opening times: Monday – Friday 11.30am – 11pm; Saturday 12pm – 11pm & Sunday hours.

Ales include: Stones, Draught Bass, Bass Mild

Bar Snacks/Meals: Yes

Range: Extensive

Live Music: No

Jukebox: Yes

Fruit Machines: Yes

Function Room: No

The Eagle Hotel in Paradise Street has had an unusual history. At different times in the last century it is reputed to have been a pawn shop, and a coffee house, and it is even thought to have operated as a brothel. These days the only needs that are catered for are nothing more notorious than those of the thirsty or the hungry.

The exterior of the alehouse is dominated by a large, black eagle, perched above the door, glaring defiantly across the street. The Eagle Hotel has quite a smart front, and the black shutters on the upstairs windows give the pub an almost continental look in the centre of Liverpool. Inside, the decoration consists of a mix between the modern and the ancient. The bar is standard and modern in design, while the surrounding area is divided into cave-like areas, with half-timbered and whitewashed walls of uneven surface. Nevertheless, here is a pleasant pub offering many quiet areas in which to enjoy a meal or a drink.

A point to note in this pub concerns the contentious issue of bar music. Music is played in this pub at a sensible level, and while it remains unobtrusive, it does tend to create a favourable atmosphere. Other licensees take note!

In summary, the Eagle Hotel is an interesting house with a curious interior, which retains its diverse and appreciative custom by virtue of the comfortable prevailing atmosphere. While not of any significant historical interest, it is a decent alehouse worthy of a visit.

The Empire

70 Hanover Street

Opening times: Monday – Saturday, 11.30am – 11pm; Closed Sundays.

Ales include: Cains, Tetley

Bar Snacks/Meals: No

Live Music: Yes

Jukebox: Yes

Fruit Machines: Yes

Function Room: No

The Empire in Hanover Street appears to be a rather run-down corner house from the street outside, but on entering, it shows the obvious signs of recent revamping. In fact, it was refurbished two years ago so that nowadays, it is a clean and pleasant alehouse to linger in, probably unrecognisable to anyone who knew the pub twenty or thirty years ago.

The Empire is known among the locals as "Tracy's". While the pub has always been called the Empire, it is called "Tracy's" after an old landlord who owned the house around thirty years ago. In those days, the pub had a very high bar counter to prevent the patrons from talking to the barmaids, which Tracy presumably thought meant lost business. The bar then used to have several different snug areas. These days, it is open plan, with a bar of average height. Decoration is 'standard pub interior', but there is quite an attractive fireplace towards the rear of the pub, with a large wooden surround holding a clock above.

The Empire is said to be a haunted pub, according to an old local. There is apparently an old man who inhabits uninvited the accommodation upstairs, though it seems that most pubs in Liverpool can offer some sort of unearthly presence these days.

The Empire is a decent sort of pub, but one feels that perhaps the recent renovations have been to the dislike of an older set of drinkers; the character of the old house has gone. It remains, however, an agreeable alehouse that benefits from its central location.

The Excelsior

121/123 Dale Street

Opening times: Monday – Wednesday 11.30am – 3pm; 5pm – 11pm; Thursday – Friday 11.30am – 11pm; Closed Saturday & Sunday.

Ales include: Cains, Higsons, Theakstons

Bar Snacks/Meals: Yes

Range: Extensive

Live Music: No

Jukebox: Yes

Fruit Machines: Yes

Function Room: Yes

The Excelsior is a compact, serviceable pub by an inelegant flyover that fortunately does not detract from the smart red-brick exterior. Despite being on the 'wrong' end of Dale Street, it is a popular daytime pub, catering for many businessmen and locals, lending to the pub the pleasing bustle of weekday lunchtimes.

The interior is split into two parts, with a U-shaped bar area, and a large room to the side. The décor consists of the flock wallpaper and high, cream ceilings that are reminiscent of turn-of-the-century prosperity. Glass light shades hang from the ceiling, while the large room to the side has a panelled far wall and panelled ceiling that complement the stylish interior. The Excelsior has a spacious, comfortable design, although it has perhaps a slightly worn-at-the-edges feel about it.

The Excelsior has an unusual history, almost a 'double life', considering that the original building that housed the pub was demolished to make way for a car park. The Excelsior now occupies the site of a previous pub called the 'Old Scotch House', which in the 1911 Liverpool Directory is listed at 123 Dale Street, with the original Excelsior at 121. Apparently, large ornamental stone thistles were removed from the top of the building to make way for the Excelsior, but it is not known where these are now.

It seems a shame that one pub must disappear to make way for another. Indeed, the 'Old Scotch House' sounds like some iniquitous drinking-den worthy of notoriety. At least with the Excelsior we can console ourselves in a pub of some distinction.

Flanagan's Apple

18 Mathew Street

Opening times: Monday – Wednesday, 11.30am – 12am; Thursday – Saturday, 11.30am – 2am & Sunday hours.

Ales include: Pedigree, Marstons' Best

Bar Snacks/Meals: Yes

Range: Extensive

Live Music: Yes (every night)

Jukebox: Traditional Irish Folk (loud)

Fruit Machines: Yes

Function Room: Yes

"Liverpool is the pool of life"
C.G. Jung, 1927. [Inscription on the outside wall]

Flanagan's Apple can probably be described as one of Liverpool city centre's most popular alehouses, successfully and tastefully combining a traditional Irish atmosphere with the diverse influence of Liverpool's seafaring history. "Flannies", as it is known, attracts people from all walks of life, young and old, and is quite popular with the student fraternity particularly on Friday and Saturday evenings, when the live music in the basement bar, usually Irish and Liverpudlian folk songs, is most widely appreciated.

Flanagan's Apple is in one of the huge fruit merchants' warehouses that line Mathew Street. It is a large alehouse, with three floors. The ground floor is the main bar area, and is a wonderfully atmospheric place for a drink any time of the day. With bare floorboards and wooden fittings throughout, it houses many artifacts from a Liverpool now gone. While there are tables and chairs along the walls, at busy times many people stand around the large barrels placed around the floor, to be used as tables. During the day, Irish folk is played in here. Upstairs, there is a restaurant area, open only during the daytime, which has its own bar. The basement bar has a small

26

stage, and it is here that the best of the Apple's unique ambience can be sampled. The live performances are fairly informal and appreciated by everybody.

Noisy and crowded, or relaxed and sociable depending on the time of day, Flanagan's Apple remains a firm favourite with many local drinkers, and preserves the inimitable nightlife along this most historic street in Liverpool.

The Globe Hotel

17 Cases Street

Opening times: Monday – Saturday, 11am – 11pm & Sunday hours.

Ales include: Cains, Higsons.

Bar Snacks/Meals: No

Live Music: No

Jukebox: Yes

Fruit Machines: Yes

Function Room: No

The Globe Hotel stands in Cases Street, a stout, impressive building that seems incongruous with the modernity of Clayton Square nearby. It is a rather quaint alehouse, displaying a sculptured globe in the eaves of the roof. It is listed in the Liverpool Directory as having been a spirit dealer's premises, but from 1859 it appears as 'The Globe'. The building it now occupies dates from 1888.

The Globe is a very small, friendly pub, often frequented by a set of characters fond of their ale. It can be crowded and noisy at most times of the day, and it tends to attract the archetypal 'preacher of doom', who is willing to tout his political and religious theories to anyone in earshot. Some refuge can be found in the tiny snug area at the back, which has space for about ten people, but which normally holds no more than two

or three. Here, newspapers line the walls recording various exploits and operations during the Second World War.

The Globe is noted for its idiosyncratic sloping floor that has the tendency to project patrons towards the street, a blessing at times, but which can be disconcerting depending on one's level of inebriation. The bar itself is long and thin, with an attractive stained glass surround overhead. While there are tables and chairs available around the bar, it seems that most drinkers prefer to stand.

This is a friendly, likeable alehouse, definitely unique. It has a smart interior having been refurbished in 1988, and is worth a stop in the late afternoon, to escape the oppressiveness of the city outside.

The Grapes

25 Mathew Street

Opening times: Monday – Saturday, 12pm – 11pm; Closed Sunday.

Ales include: Cains, Higsons

Bar Snacks/Meals: Yes

Range: Good

Live Music: No

Jukebox: Yes

Fruit Machines: Yes

Function Room: No

At the turn of the century, the Grapes in Mathew Street shared its address with a fruit merchant's shop, an old coach house and then a grocer's shop. It was originally called 'The Commercial', and it is said that an alehouse of some description has been on the site for over 300 years, although the large fruit merchant's warehouses that line Mathew Street are of a more recent time.

It could be said that the prime of the Grapes' life to date was back in the 1960s, when the Beatles drank there and the house was known as "The Beatles' Pub". This is not hard to believe when you consider that they were quite a bit older than the adolescent, tee-total audiences that they played to, and consequently had to find places other than the Cavern to quench their thirsts. It was here as well that Pete Best drowned his sorrows after his sacking from the band in 1962.

What is harder to believe is a story the present landlord related, of how President William Clinton, a confirmed Beatles' fan, apparently visited the Grapes during his time at Oxford, and stepped in to stop a fight between Ringo Starr and some inebriated young delinquent: not for the only time the US presidency assumes a peacemaking role!

The Grapes has undergone a sensitive refurbishment, and an extension in the early 1980s, so that today it is an attractive and a very popular watering hole. Beamed ceilings are in evidence throughout, and the whole place has an intimate 'nook and cranny' feel about it. During the winter months, an open fire blazes in one part of the pub, with the cheery glow of an old stove alight in another. It can get quite crowded on weekend evenings, but then it is only at these times that Mathew Street really comes alive.

The Hanover

Hanover Street

Opening times: Monday – Saturday, 11.30am – 11pm; Sunday 7pm – 10.30pm

Ales include: Courage Directors, John Smith, Websters.

Bar Snacks/Meals: Yes

Range: Extensive

Live Music: No

Jukebox: Yes

Fruit Machines: Yes

Function Room: No

The Hanover is on Hanover Street, near Ranelagh Street. It is an attractive building, and the exterior of darkened glass and whitewashed walls is quite different to what one would expect of a city centre alehouse. A cask hangs over the doorway announcing the sale of "real ales", which is always a promising sign.

Inside, it is soon clear that the pub is very modern, and also very large. The open plan design produces a huge bar area, but there are several different areas and rooms off the bar. The rooms to the left of the bar as one walks in are raised slightly above the level of the bar area, and at lunchtime are given over to diners who have their meals brought to the table.

The first of these rooms is well-decorated and features technical drawings of various ships, liners and the like. Unusual elements of the decoration, common through the whole pub, are the stuffed birds and fish. What significance these bear is not known other than to create a general feeling of old country goodness, but it is certainly a taxidermist's dream!

The interior is perhaps a little overdone, with brass lights and ceiling fans but it is a clean and attractive pub that attracts a fair amount of custom. Those preferring a little more of the traditional alehouse atmosphere can find a smoking room to the right of the bar, behind the entrance, which holds a couple of pool tables.

The Hanover is a decent pub that attracts many young families. Unfortunately, young children tend to roam loose at times which is certainly not to the liking of all drinkers.

The Lion Tavern

67 Moorfields (corner of Tithebarn Street)
Opening times: Monday – Saturday, 12pm – 11pm; Closed Sunday.
Ales include: Walkers Bitter and Mild
Bar Snacks/Meals: Yes
Range: Extensive
Live Music: No
Jukebox: Yes
Fruit Machines: Yes
Function Room: No

The Lion Tavern in Moorfields is named after the early locomotive, from the 1890s, that worked on the Manchester to Liverpool railway. It stands roughly opposite the now closed Exchange Street station, which is why it is named so.

The Lion is an ornate Victorian alehouse, and the lavishness of detail associated with this type of house is immediately apparent on the outside of the building. Proud moulded lions are featured in the decoration above door height, and the large frosted windows produce in total, the effect reminiscent of a cosy, Victorian house.

Inside the pub, the splendour of the decoration is continued. The bar is in the centre of the alehouse, and there are different areas projecting from it on all sides. The main areas consist of a public bar at the front of the pub with coloured tiles covering the walls, and two parlours towards the rear. In one of these parlours, there is a notable fireplace with a copper surround that makes the room a very pleasant place to enjoy a good lunch. The alehouse also features an imposing glass dome set into the ceiling, allowing light to flood through it and to illuminate the room beneath.

The Lion Tavern is a satisfying house that is regularly enjoyed for its very reasonable lunchtime menu. It is a listed building, which can give us some idea of the impressive architecture that improves this corner of Tithebarn Street. It is frequented most often by the office workers from the extensive business section across the street who, presented with the Lion Tavern and the Railway Hotel, have a better class of pub in which to spend a lunchtime, or enjoy a drink after work. Those who have never ventured into this part of the centre should do so.

The Liverpool

14 James Street

Opening times: Monday – Saturday, 11am – 11pm & Sunday hours.

Ales include: Tetley Bitter and Mild

Bar Snacks/Meals: Yes

Range: Extensive

Live Music: Yes

Jukebox: Yes

Fruit Machines: Yes

Function Room: No

The Liverpool in James Street takes its name from the destroyer that was launched from Cammell Laird's shipyard just over ten years ago, although it had already had several previous names, including 'The Mona' and 'The James'. It is renowned for being an old seafarers' alehouse and it is said that past and present crews of the Liverpool come here for a reunion every time the ship is in.

The Liverpool is near James Street station, part of the row of buildings

34

along that side of the street. It is a little scruffy from the outside these days, but it still attracts a good crowd during the daytime always ready to raise a smile. The house used to have three floors with three different bars in operation, but these days there are only two that are used- the Douglas Bar and the Manx Bar. The interior has seen better days, but it is a relaxed pub with friendly staff.

Some confusion exists as to when the pub was first opened. Apparently, a pub on this site was bombed during the Second World War so perhaps that explains why the pub was 're-opened' in the 1950s. The Liverpool is yet another of Liverpool's haunted alehouses. There is a strange presence in the cellar, according to a member of staff. A curious story that was related was that when the River Mersey is at its highest, the cellar of the house becomes flooded so that the barrels can be seen afloat. I wasn't lucky enough to see this phenomenon.

The Liverpool is an atmospheric place that retains a sizeable custom of old seafarers and is an important link with Liverpool's past. It is friendly and welcoming to all.

The Midland
Ranelagh Street
Opening times: 11am – 11pm & Sunday Hours.
Ales include: Walker's Bitter, Best and Mild
Bar Snacks/Meals: Yes
Range: Average
Live Music: No
Jukebox: Yes
Fruit Machines: Yes
Function Room: No

The Midland in Ranelagh Street is next door to the Central, and while the exterior is rather grand with polished marble and well-stocked hanging baskets, the interior unfortunately bears little resemblance. Like the Central, it was originally a private dwelling before becoming a licensed house in 1875.

Inside the Midland, the fittings are not on the same scale as those of the Central. It bears the signs of recent refurbishment, which considering the age of the alehouse, and the modern appearance of the pub now, seems unforgivable. The pub is separated into different cubicles by wooden screen partitions with diner-style seating in each cubicle. To the right of the large bar area is a shelf high above the floor carrying various interesting objects that appear to have been collected over the years. There is also a clock made by 'Geo. Eccles & Son, Liverpool' who must have been commissioned by Walkers to produce several large and ornate clocks for the interiors of their pubs, considering that so many can still be seen around the city. There is an etched mirror behind the bar that perhaps is the only touch of authenticity about the interior.

The exterior of the Midland is the most notable feature of this alehouse. The beautiful front curves round from Ranelagh Street into Cases Street, and is a striking feature of the design. It is a good example of the architectural style associated with a town house towards the end of the nineteenth century.

There must have been quite an atmosphere around Cases Street and Ranelagh Street fifty years ago, considering the number of alehouses concentrated in what is only a small area. While many of these have disappeared, the Midland has stood the test of time. It seems a pity that the brewery management can so clumsily tamper with houses of such quality. At least we can still enjoy the exterior.

The Old Post Office
The Old Post Office, L1
Opening times: Monday – Saturday, 11.30am – 11pm. Closed Sundays.
Ales include: Bass Bitter and Mild, Stones and Toby Light.
Bar Snacks/Meals: Yes
Range: Limited
Live Music: No
Jukebox: Yes
Fruit Machine: Yes
Function Room: No

The Old Post Office is an authentic looking corner house. It has an "olde worlde" exterior that appears to have been untouched over the years. It stands in a quiet street just outside the centre of town, and is perhaps somewhere not very familiar to most Liverpudlians.

The outside of the alehouse is complemented by attractive globe-shaped lights that extend over the fronted windows. Once inside, however, the pub is barely recognisable compared with this authentic exterior. This is not to say that it isn't pleasant, just that it has that immediately recognisable look of recent refurbishment. It seems a shame that the interiors of pubs like the Old Post Office are not left alone, because these days there are so few examples from the beginning of the century. The interior is clean and tidy, if not over-distinguished. It consists of an average sized main bar area, with a room to the rear that is a lot quieter than the bar, where music can be played quite loudly.

Regarding the interesting features of the house, it is somewhere between 150 and 200 years old, and is another of Liverpool's many haunted alehouses where a strange presence can be felt sometimes. (Perhaps such tales serve as good sales techniques?)

It is not the most popular of city alehouses, which means that one can usually find a seat. The Old Post Office is a decent alehouse that, with a little more imagination and effort from the brewery, could be something of a treasure.

Pig and Whistle

Covent Garden

Opening times: Monday – Friday 11.30am – 11pm; Saturday 12pm – 11pm; Closed Sunday.

Ales include: Walkers Bitter and Mild and a guest

Bar Snacks/Meals: Yes

Range: Average

Live Music: No

Jukebox: No

Fruit Machines: Yes

Function Room: Yes

The Pig and Whistle in Covent Garden is a very old pub that has probably the closest connection to the seafaring history of Liverpool of any alehouse. It was at one time a chop house, but the present building is probably of a more recent date, although it is a listed building.

The Pig and Whistle used to supply emigrants with any items they needed before embarking. Indeed, an original brass sign proudly announcing 'Emigrants Supplied' can still be seen attached to the wall opposite the bar. Its name is an indication of the variety of goods that could be purchased there before the great ships set sail for North America and elsewhere.

The exterior of the pub is rather tatty these days and it seems unusually positioned with respect to the buildings around it. Thankfully, this does not correspond with the interior, which recently refurbished, is quite splendid. There are several different rooms on different levels. The main bar area is reached by climbing some steps from the street, while to the left is a small room that houses a large clock reached by a few more stairs. Finally, there is a room upstairs with its own bar, where meals are served and consumed. The décor has a strong seafaring theme, with maps of the docks and pictures of old Liverpool appearing for once significantly in an alehouse with strong traditions. Plush red leather seats contribute to the general feeling of homeliness.

Here is an alehouse with an important place in the history of Liverpool. Our distant relatives may have passed through here before leaving for foreign lands. Let us hope the Pig and Whistle is preserved so that we may remember this important facet of life in Liverpool.

The Poste House

Cumberland Street (off Dale Street)

Opening times: Monday – Saturday, 11am – 11pm; usual Sunday hours.
Ales include: Cains Bitter & Mild, Higsons Bitter & Mild, and a guest
Bar Snacks/Meals: Yes
Range: Limited
Live Music: No
Jukebox: No (taped)
Fruit Machines: No
Function Room: Yes

The Poste House in Cumberland Street, off Dale Street, is a fascinating alehouse by virtue of its rich historical background. It is a tiny and homely pub, in a dark, quiet back street that belies the gratifying nature of this house.

From outside, the Poste House displays a thin, weathered front that lends an authenticity to its reputed history. Inside, it is a cosy, warming place with two small rooms on two floors. Downstairs is the main bar, and it is here that during the day most of the drinkers can be found. The upstairs bar is reached by the staircase on the back wall, this room opening in the afternoon to provide more seating. The interior is quite delightful, the ground floor room having a fireplace surrounded by pictures of a Liverpool of old. The downstairs bar is in the corner of the room to the left of the door, and it has attractive stained glass screens around the top. The upstairs room is decorated in a similar manner, but with pictures of racehorses adorning the walls.

The Poste House has played host to a horde of famous and infamous people in the past, if we are to believe the stories that exist. If the alleged references in his diaries are to be believed, Jack the Ripper made a visit to the Poste House at some time in the latter part of the nineteenth century, as did William Thackeray, the distinguished English author, although it is not suggested that they were members of the same drinking party!

The alehouse is reputed to have been the haunt of smugglers, but these days we must make do with a mere haunting: the ghostly figure of a woman is said to stand at the top of the stairs.

The Poste House is a welcoming and interesting little house that is worth visiting, whether one believes the stories or not. It all adds some flavour to the beer!

The Queens Hotel

Derby Square

Opening times: Monday – Saturday, 11am – 11pm & Sunday hours.

Ales include: Bass Bitter.

Bar Snacks/Meals: Yes

Range: Average

Live Music: Yes (Sunday, Tuesday, Friday)

Jukebox: Yes

Fruit Machines: Yes

Function Room: No

The Queens in Derby Square occupies a modern concrete building and consequently is of no great architectural interest. However, it is a popular city centre alehouse that attracts a good deal of passing trade, and in this respect is worthy of some attention.

It is named after Queen Victoria, standing as it does opposite a huge memorial bearing a statue of a very proud-looking Victoria. There are separate figures depicting some of the exploits of the British nation, and of Liverpool, under her rule. It is close to the imposing law courts in Derby Square and not too far from James Street Station.

Inside the Queens, the pub is divided into two areas, to the left and to the right of the door. The interior is decorated in a standard fashion. On the whole, the atmosphere is very relaxed inside, and it seems to attract the older Liverpudlian. This may be due to the connections that exist with an older Liverpool. There are separate displays on the walls, featuring collections of knots and stamps that indicate Liverpool's seafaring history as one of the great world ports. Indeed, several retired seaman drink in this area and in the Queens itself; maybe something to do with it being close to the river, and the smell of the sea air.

One small grumble is with the television and the jukebox in the main bar area, Both are quite obtrusive, and have the effect

43

of dampening the conversation around the bar, It appears to be the rule nowadays that a bar must play music, but this can be relaxing rather than an intrusion. Televisions are a distraction, and rarely have a place in the alehouse.

The Railway Hotel
18 Tithebarn Street
Opening times: Monday – Saturday, 11.30am – 11pm & Sunday hours.
Ales include: Boddingtons, Cains Bitter & Mild
Bar Snacks/Meals: Yes
Range: Extensive
Live Music: No
Jukebox: Yes
Fruit Machines: Yes
Function Room: Yes

The Railway in Tithebarn Street is a striking pub when viewed from outside. The smart black exterior, complimented by well-stocked hanging baskets, make an impressive visage. The Railway stands opposite the old Exchange Street station, where some of the first locomotives entered Liverpool from Manchester, and duly takes its name from its locality. The windows of the alehouse are quite notable, halved and in stained glass depicting various scenes of the railway, such as the Exchange station and the Flying Scotsman.

Inside, what is immediately striking is the sheer lavishness of decoration. The ceiling is superb, encrusted with floral designs, and with large stately lights hanging intermittently. The bar itself is spacious, curving round the room, with an attractive coloured glass screen surrounding the top announcing 'The Railway Hotel'. On the wall facing the bar is a large clock housed in an ornate carved casing reminiscent of a station clock, while the railway theme is continued in all other areas around the bar, predictably with photographs of different railway scenes.

The Railway is a very popular pub at lunchtime, and rightly so. It is an example to all those in brewery management of how a pub can be sensitively refurbished, with consideration shown to the patron and to the historical value of the alehouse. Right in the centre of the business section of Liverpool between

Tithebarn Street and Dale Street, it is the venue for many working lunches, but it also remains popular with a local element. Let us hope such sound traditions are continued.

The Richmond

32 Williamson Street

Opening times: Monday – Saturday, 11am – 11pm & Sunday hours.

Ales include: Bass Bitter

Bar Snacks/Meals: No

Live Music: No

Jukebox: Yes

Fruit Machines: Yes

Function Room: No

The Richmond near Williamson Square is a well-frequented alehouse, situated as it is in the centre of the shopping precinct. Because it has only a tiny bar, drinkers are stood outside on the precinct at most times. It is the archetypal 'city house', attracting drinkers from all over, creating a typically Liverpudlian atmosphere.

The Richmond is a corner house, smartly decorated in a red and blue scheme. Inside, the tiny bar area appears full at most times of the day, and is frequented by a regular set of drinkers that give rise to some spirited conversation. The bar has a tiled floor and authentic ships lanterns hanging from the ceiling, and while unremarkable, is of a clean and serviceable appearance. Through the bar to the right is a lounge room, a snug that offers much quieter and relaxed surroundings, although this itself is very small, with seating for about up to about 20 drinkers.

The Richmond is another of Liverpool's reputedly haunted alehouses. It is said that the presence of an old landlord called A.H. Simatt can be felt about the bar. This may have something to do with the possession of an old nameplate bearing his name, that used to hang above the bar.

The Richmond is typical of a good deal of Liverpool alehouses; unspectacular, but well adjusted to service the needs of the community. However, while other inner city houses have become decrepit, the Richmond remains a clean and tidy place to enjoy a pint, amid the heat and the dust of the city.

Rigby's

23-25 Dale Street

Opening times: 11am – 11pm except Sundays.
Ales include: Higsons
Bar Snacks/Meals: Yes
Live Music: Yes (Monday)
Range: Extensive
Jukebox: Yes
Fruit Machines: Yes
Function Room: Yes

Rigby's stands on Dale Street, perched ostentatiously at the top of North John Street. It occupies the ground floor of the magnificent Rigby's Buildings which date from 1726, and give to the pub an unusual aspect of faded elegance. Although formerly known as 'The George', an alehouse has existed on the site since 1726.

On closer inspection, the exterior of the buildings alludes to the affluence created when Liverpool was a great, bustling port. Inside, there are two bars, the Trafalgar Bar and the Cellar Bar, with a snug behind called the Nelson Room. The Nelson Room is a peculiar room that seems to bear a closer resemblance to a cabinet office than to an alehouse snug. This austere impression is created by the extensive oak panelling and velvet upholstery which presumably resulted from the renovation and refurbishment in 1922 by Ashby Tabb Ltd, according to an inscription above the fireplace.

The Nelson Room, the most interesting feature of this pub, is a spacious, square room with a fireplace to the right of the door, and an impressive painting of Nelson's ship Victory on the far wall. It is unsure why this room is named after the great admiral, but one salacious theory suggests that there once took place here an amorous meeting of Lord Nelson and Lady Hamilton. Rigby's has in its time housed various items of Nelson memorabilia, including a contract bearing the admiral's own handwriting, but whether the great man ever visited is very debatable.

Rigby's is an attractive pub, if perhaps a little neglected, which retains many of its original features, such as the painted carvings on the lintels. It is a popular city centre pub which unfortunately, and to its detriment, has acquired a jukebox. Such progress seems strangely anachronistic in eighteenth century surroundings.

Rose and Crown

7 Cheapside (off Dale Street)

Opening times: Monday – Saturday, 12pm – 11pm & Sunday hours.
Ales include: Worthingtons, Cains Bitter, Bass Mild
Bar Snacks/Meals: Yes
Range: Good
Live Music: No
Jukebox: No
Fruit Machines: Yes
Function Room: No

The Rose and Crown in Cheapside off Dale Street has recently been refurbished, and these days offers townsfolk and workers from the business quarter a pleasant spot for lunch. It has a smart, rather squat, appearance from outside, and sports a large Union Jack and hanging baskets. It does much to improve an otherwise shabby back street.

The interior of the pub is clean and comfortable, with accommodating red velvet chairs and benches lining the walls. Despite being only of an average size, etched mirrors on the far wall of the bar give the appearance of a much larger pub. The ambience of this pub is quite relaxed and welcoming.

When we consider the history of the Rose and Crown, not much in the way of firm evidence exists, mostly hearsay. It has been said that several conspirators met on this site, their plotting leading to civil war. This war was presumably the War of the Roses, given the name of the pub. Another story exists claiming that at some time in the nineteenth century, a group of bishops met here to discuss the merits of a number of candidates for the papacy. If there is an element of truth in either story, the Rose and Crown is certainly quite old, and historically quite interesting.

The Rose and Crown attracts the lunchtime trade of businessmen and women, as is common among the houses near Dale Street. It is an agreeable pub that caters well for its passing trade.

Rosie O'Grady's

Hanover Street
Opening times: Vary
Ales include: Marston's Pedigree
Bar Snacks/Meals: Yes
Range: Extensive
Live Music: Yes
Jukebox: Yes
Fruit Machines: Yes
Function Room: Yes

Rosie O'Grady's, like Flanagan's Apple, has brought a traditional Irish atmosphere to the centre of Liverpool in an attempt to appeal to the same large numbers of people that the 'Apple' does. It stands on the corner of Hanover Street and Wood Street, occupying a huge old warehouse, like a monolith from a time long past.

Steps lead down from the street into the bar which, it is soon apparent, is not at all dissimilar to the ground floor bar of Flanagan's. In similar fashion, the décor is the most basic, appealing in a ruggedly charming way, with bare floors, old wooden tables and pews, and with various olde worlde artifacts dotted around for extra effect. It has the feeling of being a good deal younger, and less used, than Flanagan's – which of course it is. This detracts from its supposed authenticity.

Rosie O'Grady's has a late licence most evenings, which means it can stay open like a club. In this way, it is appealing to those who would want to drink well into the night, without the obligation of having to pay to get into a club. The live entertainment is a mixture of traditional and modern folk, pleasing to listen to and guaranteed to produce a spirited atmosphere. It is interesting that the 'folk night' is staging something of a come-back after the nihilistic 1980s, and is now promoted at many alehouses around the city, known to be a good draw.

Rosie O'Grady's is an appealing watering hole that provides an alternative to the routine of the pub or club night. It can get very busy on Friday and Saturday evenings, but then in places like this, the elbow-to-elbow factor is a good index to the atmosphere.

The Saddle Inn

13-15 Dale Street

Opening times: Monday – Thursday, 11.30am – 9pm; Friday 11.30am – 11pm; Saturday 11.30am – 4pm; 6pm – 11pm; Closed Sunday.

Ales include: Worthingtons, Cains Bitter, Bass Mild

Bar Snacks/Meals: Yes

Range: Extensive

Live Music: No

Jukebox: No

Fruit Machines: Yes

Function Room: No

The Saddle Inn in Dale Street, while not remarkable among the houses in the area, is a refreshing pub with a gentle, relaxing daytime atmosphere. It was previously called 'The Palatine', presumably because of the link with Thomas Henry Ismay (1837-1899) who founded the Oceanic Steam Navigation Company which, under its famous White Star Line flag, was the most powerful shipping line company in the North Atlantic.

The Saddle stands smartly on the corner of Dale Street and Hackins Hey. Inside, the bar is to the right of the door, and there is a central pillar dividing the seating area. Restful green leather seating complements the interior and it has a most urbane setting in what is probably at its best as an 'afternoon house'. The shipping link is continued in the bar with pictures of liners and old scenes of Liverpool life on the walls.

A notice in the bar describes how Thomas Ismay "kept up

an angry exchange of letters with his cousin John Sealby at the Old Saddle Hotel in Dale Street which stood near the site of the present pub." This 'angry exchange' concerned John Sealby's management of one of the vessels, the 'Charles Bronwell', which Ismay thought was irresponsible.

The Saddle is a comfortable alehouse, popular within the business quarter, and worth a visit in the late afternoon to sample the relaxed atmosphere.

The Slaughterhouse

15 Fenwick Street

Opening times: Monday – Thursday, 11am – 11pm; Friday & Saturday, 11am – 2am; Closed Sunday.

Ales include: Marston's Best and Pedigree, London Pride

Bar Snacks/Meals: Yes

Range: Extensive

Live Music: Yes (Wed)

Jukebox: Yes

Fruit Machines: Yes

Function Room: No

The Slaughterhouse in Fenwick Street has very definite claims to be the oldest licensed house in Liverpool. It has had an uncertain past, and it is only recently that it was re-opened following a five year period of closure. Nowadays, it is an interesting place to drink in the old business district of Liverpool.

The pub began life as a wine merchant's store, and still displayed on the walls outside is a record of this: 'George Bennett & Sons, Wine & Spirit Merchants'. The primary function of this store was in the import and delivery of fine wines, but there was also a tiny room attached to the main operations that served draught Bass. This had to close at 3 o'clock in the afternoon because technically it was a shop. It was this tiny bar that represents the beginning of the Slaughterhouse's long life as an alehouse.

The Corn Exchange used to be very close to Fenwick Street, and it has been said that more business was done in the Slaughterhouse than was ever done in the Exchange. Corn and barley and maize used to be trodden all the time, since the floor was covered with grain. Back in the days before cooling systems, grass sods used to be placed over the barrels of ale in the summer to keep them cool, while in the winter sacks were piled on top of them to keep them free of frost. The Slaughterhouse has been the haunt of a variety of people ranging from dockers to professionals from the business district of the city. The cosmopolitan atmosphere of the house has always been maintained.

For some reason, the Slaughterhouse was converted into a winebar in the 1970s, probably when this was in vogue, and then became a restaurant/pub in the early 1980s. Following its demise, the house was closed for five years. It was re-opened in 1993, in the style of an Irish-Liverpool bar similar to Flanagan's Apple and Rosie O'Grady's, and it seems that this has fared a little better. Unfortunately though, Fenwick Street these days is not nearly as important as it used to be, and so custom has waned somewhat.

The Slaughterhouse is an agreeable place for a drink that has some original features, such as the order book from the time it operated as a wine importer. It has two floors, with the main bar set into the stone of the old warehouse walls. Despite an uncertain past, it remains one of the oldest alehouses in Liverpool, and therefore holds an important position in the history of the city.

The Swan Inn

86, Wood Street.

Opening times: Monday – Saturday, 11.30am – 11pm & Sunday hours.
Ales include: Cains Bitter, Marstons Pedigree, Wobbly Bob and guest beers.
Bar Snacks/Meals: Yes
Range: Average
Live Music: Yes
Jukebox: Yes
Fruit Machines: Yes
Function Room: No

The Swan Inn is an unusual city centre alehouse, situated down a dark and dingy back street in an old part of Liverpool. It has an authentic, traditional front that suggests a seedy drinking den, but really it couldn't be further from the truth. The Swan attracts a large, friendly crowd at most times. It has a reputation for being something of a bikers' pub which, in my experience, explains its friendly atmosphere, although it does seem odd for a bikers' pub to be so central.

The interior of the Swan is very pleasant, with beamed ceilings, original wooden floorboards and copper-topped tables. There are pictures on the walls ranging from Marilyn Monroe to works of modern art, and there is a good selection of photographs of old Liverpool. The downstairs bar is just one large room with various tables around the bar. The back of this room feels rather cave-like, and houses an old jukebox. There is also an upstairs section to the bar, and there is a tale about its origins. Apparently in the 1950s, it was opened by a female brothel owner at the suggestion of her husband to put her ill-gotten gains into something worthwhile. Her husband was a racing driver, which is the reason the upstairs bar is called "The Steering Wheel". A fire in the 1950s destroyed the downstairs area, which used to have three separate rooms and two bars.

It was said that for the size of it, the Swan Inn once sold the most ale in the country. Whether this is true or not, it is certainly not an alehouse for a quick drink; people have been known to spend days in here! Overall, the Swan is a real surprise, a delight that perhaps only a handful of regulars know of, and definitely a place to look out for.

The Vines
81, Lime Street

Opening times: Monday – Saturday, 11am – 11pm; usual Sunday hours.
Ales include: Walker's Beers.
Bar Snacks/Meals: Yes
Range: Extensive
Live Music: No
Jukebox: Yes
Fruit Machines: Yes
Function Room: Yes

The Vines in Lime Street rivals the Philharmonic as the most splendid, grandiose alehouse in Liverpool, if not the whole of the country. Similarly to the 'Phil', it was designed by Walter Thomas, architect to the brewer Robert Cain, as an extraordinary 'gin palace' in the style of exuberant Edwardian Baroque. Really, it is difficult to decide whether the grand exterior is more impressive then the plush interior.

The Vines, also known as the 'Big House', stands on the site of an alehouse dating from 1813, although it was rebuilt in 1907 to Thomas' design. It was constructed for Mr Walker, the brewer, designed to carry and display his favourite paintings, some of which remain. Further renovations were carried out by the brewery in 1989, which sadly saw the removal of a small parlour and an original Edwardian WC.

Outside, the pub is resplendent, with carved stone and marble forming a most extravagant visage. There is a large

clock extending from the outside face on Lime Street that was manufactured by the same company that built Big Ben. The Vines is a most imposing corner house. Inside, the opulence of the interior is expressed with mahogany pillars and carved fittings throughout. The house consists of three separate areas: two bar areas, and a magnificent function room, called the 'Heritage Suite' to the rear. This impressive room is centred on a superb stained glass cupola, encrusted with rosebuds around the rim, and surrounded by a beautifully panelled ceiling. Before the 1960s, this used to be a billiard room, with a small bar, but it was renovated, the bar was extended, and large portraits now hang in their producing in total such a palatial interior. The other bar areas, while not so lavish, both have striking fireplaces, one of which features carved statuettes around a marble hearth.

The Vines is a wonderfully stately alehouse that, it has been said, represents 'an expression of the confident wealth of a world port'. It is an alehouse of which Liverpool can be justly proud.

The White Star

2 Rainford Gardens (by Mathew Street)

Opening times: Monday – Saturday, 11am – 11pm; usual Sunday hours.

Ales include: Bass, Cains, Worthingtons and a guest

Bar Snacks/Meals: Yes

Range: Limited

Live Music: Yes (Wednesday & Sunday)

Jukebox: No

Fruit Machines: Yes

Function Room: Yes

The White Star near Mathew Street is a wonderful locals' pub that is well-known throughout the city as 'a shrine for Bass drinkers'. It is named after the White Star shipping line, and connections with the seafaring past of Liverpool are evident throughout the bar.

The White Star has a smart, compact build viewed from outside, and it stands proudly on the most famous street in Liverpool. Inside, the pub is composed of two different areas: the main bar area at the front, which has a U-shaped bar in the centre, and a room off the bar at the back that used to be a dining room, but now houses a piano and expansive red leather seats. At the front of the pub, beneath the windows, there are several partially screened areas that provide several snug-like areas. It seems, however, that most of the local crowd prefer to stand at the bar, closer to the spirited conversation, and the next pint.

The Star's seafaring association has led to the bar displaying many pieces of shipping memorabilia, including pictures of different liners and a letter from the Blue Star line accepting somebody's resignation with regret: off to join the White Star no doubt! There is also a section dedicated to the local boxing fraternity from years past, with apparently one or two of the city's distinguished pugilists still drinking in the alehouse.

The White Star is a popular and friendly beer drinkers' pub. The atmosphere is welcoming, although the clientele does seem to be very male dominated, so it may not be the best place for an intimate drink.

Ye Hole in Ye Wall

Hackins Hey (off Dale Street)

Opening times: Monday – Thursday, 11.30am – 3pm; Friday & Saturday, 11.30am – 11pm; Closed Sunday.

Ales include: Walker's Bitter, Tetley, Bass

Bar Snacks/Meals: Yes

Range: Average

Live Music: No

Jukebox: Yes

Fruit Machines: Yes

Function Room: Yes

'Ye Hole in Ye Wall', as the name suggests, is a very old alehouse dating from around the beginning of the eighteenth century. It stands on the site of an original Quaker's meeting house of 1706 although the building that now houses the pub dates from 1726. It is an arresting building with half-timbered exterior that gives the touch of authenticity.

A placard inside the alehouse tells us more about the history of the pub. It states that, while records are not readily available, a headstone in St. Peter's churchyard discovered 50 years ago indicates that it was the last resting place of a sailor who was killed here, during a fight with a press gang. Also, we are told that Ye Hole in Ye Wall was one of several houses which, many years ago, were ordered to hang out their lanterns and lighted candles during the dark months of the year, since there was "no sewerage, scavenging or paving" in those days.

Ye Hole in Ye Wall is a well-preserved place, the beautiful interior a testament to that. It is divided into several separate areas, each offering a snug-like compartment for a group of drinkers. There is an ornate copper canopy in the heart of the bar, dated 'MDCCXXVI' which has lasted these years well. There is much dark- stained timber in evidence throughout the bar, contrasting with the plain painted walls. A curious feature of this alehouse is the location of the beer cellar. It is upstairs,

63

so that the beer is drawn from a tap rather than a pump. Daily newspapers hang from a rack, which is always a welcome touch.

Ye Hole in Ye Wall is a marvellous house, a gem set in the heart of the city. It has claims to be one of the oldest licensed houses in Liverpool, and it is recommended to all who may never have enjoyed this treasure.

Around the Centre and further afield

The Albert
Anfield
Opening times: Monday – Saturday, 11am – 11pm; usual Sunday hours.
Ales include: Bass Bitter
Bar Snack/Meals: No
Live Music: No
Jukebox: Yes
Fruit Machines: Yes
Function Room: No

The Albert is an alehouse well-known to many fans of Liverpool Football Club. It stands close to the hallowed turf of Anfield, the revered home of the most successful side in British football history. It is a compact place and although it is not particularly distinguished, the stylish red-brick exterior is complemented by the smart arched black edging around the lower windows.

Being so close to Anfield, the Albert is a new experience on match days when hundreds of fans pack themselves in for the pre-match warm-up, usually undertaken with some vigour. At other times, the atmosphere is considerably quieter – a popular locals' pub right in the centre of an expansive residential area.

The interior is not particularly remarkable; it is simply a decent serviceable alehouse in the heart of the city. There are two main areas, in front and behind the bar. The back area

holds a pool table, and is the haunt of younger men from around the area. The front bar, with red tiled floor, is where the old c h a r a c t e r s gather to discuss football, religion and other such important topics.

Over the years, the Albert has played host to quite a few celebrities, particularly from the footballing world, including Sir Bobby Charlton, although the presence of an ex-Manchester United player would do little to impress most regulars of this pub!

When Anfield stands empty, the Albert is a quiet place, with a rather subdued atmosphere. It is only on match days that this alehouse takes on its unique persona, and it is at these times that it is at its most enjoyable.

The Baltic Fleet
33 Wapping

Opening times: Monday – Saturday, 11am – 11pm; usual Sunday hours.
Ales include: McEwans, Youngers and guest beers
Bar Snacks/Meals: Yes
Range: Average
Live Music: No
Jukebox: Yes
Fruit Machines: Yes
Function Room: Yes

The Baltic Fleet is an unusual alehouse, situated somewhat away from the centre, along Wapping and opposite the famous, rejuvenated Albert Dock. It stands prominently at an angle to the road and it affords a remarkable vista of the dock, the River Mersey and the Wirral peninsula in the distance. It is a bit of an anomaly as pubs go really; there is some unspecifiable feature of the house that produces its unique appeal.

The striking characteristic of the exterior is that the house has been built in the shape of a ship. The collection of square chimneys, painted after the funnels of an ocean-going liner along with the flagpoles and the overall shape of the building, with obvious bow and stern, provide the nautical appearance. Quite a sight, really.

The Baltic Fleet has a stuccoed facade, all arches and pediments. Despite the early indications of neglect, here is an alehouse the city can rejoice in; an original from the mid- to late-nineteenth century that we would do well to preserve.

Inside, the Baltic Fleet appreciates a smaller custom then twenty years or so ago. It looks a little worn at the edges these days, rather like the exterior, but still functioning as a decent alehouse. It was for a long while the haunt of seamen and dockers, but these days such occupations no longer dominate the lives of Liverpudlians. The shift away from the docks on this side of the city probably explains the reduction in passing

67

trade. One can only hope that enough people continue to patronise this venerable old house, so that its long and distinguished life may be preserved.

The Grapes

60, Roscoe Street

Opening times: Monday – Saturday, 11am – 11pm; usual Sunday hours.
Ales include: Boddingtons, Cains Bitter and F.A., Higsons and Theakstons
Bar Snacks/Meals: Yes
Range: Limited
Live Music: Yes
Jukebox: Yes
Fruit Machines: Yes
Function Room: No

The Grapes on Roscoe Street is a delightful city centre alehouse, a pub that once visited will always be remembered. It was first licensed in 1897, with one William Jones becoming the first licensee on 1 March of that year. In the Victorian era, pubs were often named after their licensees so it is likely that the Grapes was known locally in the early days as Jones's. It was originally owned by James Mellor, of Mellor-off-license fame.

The interior of The Grapes is laid out in a very relaxed manner and it seems that many people like to sit at the bar to enjoy the conversation, especially during the daytime. The staff are very friendly, and always willing to share a joke or a story. Indeed, the present landlady has prepared a short history of The Grapes, and tells of an old customer of the pub, a George White, who was Lord Mountbatten's butler. It is said that a blow on his mouth-organ in this alehouse would signify a stay-behind to all in the know!

This pub is really an integral part of the local community, as can be seen from the work for charity it does. Old library books are sold to raise money for local causes, while on one day of the year there is an annual hobby-horse race between the pubs in the area.

The Grapes is a lovely pub that has its own special, warm atmosphere. There are some nice touches to the interior decoration, such as the old peanut vending machines on the walls and various other artifacts from days gone by. It is a simple, friendly place: an alehouse to note.

The Oxford

67, Oxford Street
Opening times: Vary
Ales include: Higsons Bitter, Cains Bitter
Bar Snacks/Meals: Yes
Range: Average
Live Music: No
Jukebox: Yes
Fruit Machines: Yes
Function Room: No

The Oxford is immediately striking for its position: it stands alone, isolated against the distant backdrop of urban development. It is a remarkable building, a tall three-storeyed affair and very thin. While the surrounding buildings have long since been demolished, the Oxford remains, stubbornly occupying the same site it has for many years.

It has long been the favourite haunt of university students and tutors, indeed it is this section of the clientele that is largely responsible for the lively atmosphere in this pub. The Oxford is a traditional Liverpool alehouse in all the best senses, one of those cosy places where the simplicity of the design is the most refreshing feature. Such places are geared towards serving the needs of a strong, local community, which they do satisfactorily despite only basic amenities. The Oxford's unique atmosphere is derived from this: it is a good, honest alehouse.

The interior is very small, split into two areas. The front room is taken up by the bar, while in the back room several tables and chairs are provided; this is best appreciated in the winter, when an open fire blazes in the grate. The Oxford is a vibrant alehouse and it can get quite noisy with the television and jukebox to buoy up the atmosphere. But in a way they don't detract from the warm atmosphere, unlike some pubs where their presence is inappropriate. The Oxford has no pretensions, which is its most attractive feature, and it is heartily recommended to anyone in search of a unique Liverpool alehouse.

The Philharmonic

Hope Street (off Hardman Street)

Opening times: Monday – Saturday, 11am – 11pm & Sunday hours.
Ales include: Cains, Burton, Walkers Best and Bitter and guests
Bar Snacks/Meals: Yes
Range: Extensive
Live Music: No
Jukebox: Yes
Fruit Machines: Yes
Function Room: Yes

The Philharmonic in Hope Street was officially designated by the Egon Ronay Organisation as the Most Ornate Pub in England. Egon Ronay himself declared, "If a pub could be a work of art, the Philharmonic is that pub". In a word, the 'Phil' is magnificent, a grade A listed building, and must be one of the most luxurious places to drink in the world.

It was designed by the architect to the brewer Robert Cain, Walter Thomas, in 1898 to 1900 as a showpiece in the style of a gentleman's club. It is described by the Liverpool Heritage Bureau as "a magnificent Art Nouveau confection of stepped gables, turrets, balconies and oriels." The rich gin palace interior reveals the collaboration of many artists and craftsmen from the University's then School of Architecture and Applied Art. It includes the work of the German-American designer Blomfield Bare, who produced the copper panels that decorate the former billiards room, and the lavish wrought iron and copper gates at the main entrance to the pub.

Other noted artists produced details of the internal and external surfaces. Sculptor Charles Allen worked on the ornate plaster caryatids (a support in the form of a carved female figure) which grace what is now the Grande Lounge. The stone carving was performed by stonemason Frank Norbury.

The Phil is perhaps most famous for the extravagant design of the gent's toilet, which is probably the most renowned toilet in the UK. Women have been known to dart inside for a look – indeed a ladies' toilet was not added until the late 1940s, such was the male-dominance of the house.

The Philharmonic is an awe-inspiring production: the result of a collaboration of expertise of the highest level in every field of construction. One cannot possibly give a comprehensive description of its magnificence here – you must visit it yourself. It represents a dazzling piece of Victorian flamboyance.

The Pilgrim
Pilgrim Street

Opening times: Monday – Saturday, 10.30am (for food) – 11pm & Sunday hours
Ales include: Castle Eden, Marston's Pedigree, Wadsworth 6X, Whitbread Trophy
Bar Snacks/Meals: Yes
Range: Extensive
Live Music: No
Jukebox: Yes
Fruit Machines: Yes
Function Room: No

The Pilgrim is a peculiar alehouse for several reasons. Even the small frontage on the cobbled street belies the vastness of the interior. A simple sign attached to the outside wall announces its presence here as a free house. It is one of those houses often passed by people assuming the worst, based on the evidence of the exterior, but in reality here is a pub of some distinction.

Inside, the ground floor covers a very large area. It has been called an air-raid shelter, but this is unfair because the plainness of the bar is really part of its uniqueness. The black brick walls behind the bar give some odd feeling of authenticity to the place. The seating is highly unusual. Separate 1960s American diner-style cubicles exist, with the added feature of a control module for the jukebox at each table. In the centre of the floor space, a long table stretches across the room. Up and around the spiral staircase on the far wall, there is a dining room and during term-time, this room is used as an overflow for the many students that pack themselves in downstairs.

The building has been used for a variety of ventures. The Liverpool Academy of Arts once used part of it as a gallery, while later it was bought by someone intending to open what was vaguely and suggestively described as an 'artistic club'. At one time, the upstairs section was also a Spanish restaurant. Nowadays, the Pilgrim is a quiet nook for a drink in the late afternoon, or the venue for boisterous lunchtime sessions. It is also an extremely popular student haunt on term-time evenings. It is so close to Ye Cracke that one should really visit both and compare notes.

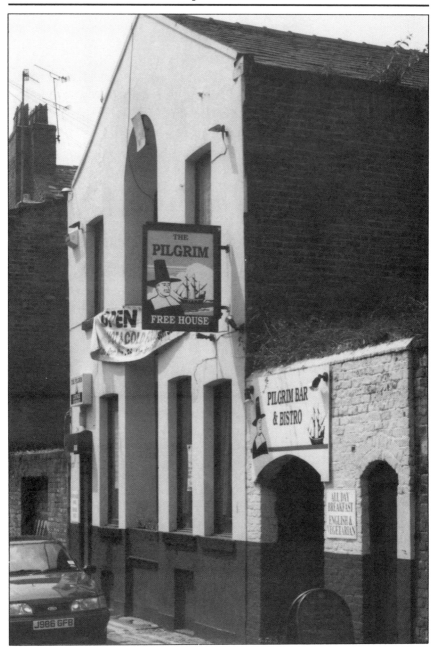

Roscoe Head

24, Roscoe Street.

Opening times: Monday – Saturday, 11am – 11pm & Sunday hours.

Ales include: Jennings, Tetley.

Bar Snacks/Meals: Yes

Range: Average

Live Music: No

Jukebox: No

Fruit Machines: No

Function Room: No

The Roscoe Head is a fine example of all that is best about Liverpool city alehouses. Situated in a back street but close to the city centre, the Roscoe Head has a dedicated section of custom that appreciates a house that has the best interests of the patrons at heart.

The alehouse is tiny, but still divided into several different areas so that a very intimate atmosphere is created. There is a very small snug behind the door just under the windows with space for only a few people, but the judicious placement of a mirror allows people to conduct conversations with others in front of the bar; ingenious use of mirrors in such a small house! There are rooms at the front of the pub and through the bar, to a very cosy parlour at the rear. A tie collection adorns the walls in this parlour, a feature the alehouse is well-known for. The regulars are very friendly – it is said the Roscoe Head is the alehouse to go to if you want a tale!

There is not much more one can say about the Roscoe Head. Its simplicity is its beauty. The decoration is not particularly outstanding, but at the same time it is a clean and smart alehouse. It is just the warmth of the place that attracts people to it, an explanation for it being the local CAMRA. Pub of the Year. It is unchanged from the alehouse it was thirty-five years ago when it was a seafarer's boozer owned by two sisters, and we can only hope it remains so. Such a successful and refreshing example of a city alehouse should survive for all to enjoy.

The Salisbury
Anfield

Opening times: Monday – Saturday, 11am – 11pm & Sunday hours
Ales include: Tetley Bitter and Mild
Bar Snacks/Meals: No
Live Music: No
Jukebox: Yes
Fruit Machines: Yes
Function Room: No

Like the Albert, the Salisbury is dominated by the presence of Liverpool Football Club a few yards down the road. When Liverpool play at home, the pub that has a complete change of character. Seemingly hundreds of fans pack themselves in sardine-like to down a few jars before kick-off. Normally, the Salisbury is a relaxed alehouse, with an atmosphere far more subdued than on those hectic days when football dominates the hearts and minds of 50% of the populace.

The building this alehouse occupies is an impressive affair, with huge gables and attractive white flagging. Inside, the interior is comfortable, if a little garish. Around the walls, pictures associated with Liverpool Football Club remind the drinker exactly where he is. Many footballers who will forever be linked with this great club appear around the bar, also "Shankly the Legend" who appears in a corner of the bar beneath the windows. Indeed, it is appropriate that the great man should be remembered in an alehouse so close to the venue for all those legendary footballing events.

The pub has an open-plan design, but there are different areas marked by screens and raised levels. It is quite a popular place even when no crowd can be heard from Anfield, and the atmosphere is friendly and welcoming as in most pubs around Liverpool. The clientele is quite mixed, with both young and old here to enjoy the ambience and the conversation. It is however on match days when the pub is at its best, and when the feeling around the bar is one of great excitement and anticipation.

The White House

185, Duke Street.

Opening times: Monday – Saturday, 11am – 11pm & Sunday 7pm – 10.30 pm

Ales include: John Smiths, Wilsons Special Mild.

Bar Snacks/Meals: Yes

Range: Limited

Live Music: Yes (Sunday, Thursday, Friday)

Jukebox: Yes

Fruit Machines: Yes

Function Room: No

The White House on Duke Street has been allowed to reach a rather shabby state, but it is a traditional working man's boozer, and quite a lot of Liverpool pubs are in this mould.

It has a fairly smart exterior, with the typical Walkers' features of polished granite lintels and the like. It stands on the corner of Duke Street and Berry Street, and though in an ideal prominent position, it has not been thought a viable proposition by the brewery.

Inside, the pub is composed of two different areas, a public bar and a lounge. The public bar to the right of the bar is called "Lynda's bar". It is small and tatty, with a pool table to one side. Small circular tables are dotted around the room, and there is a television for viewing sporting events and other spirited alehouse activities.

The pub offers cups of Oxo, hot pies and tea for its customers, and from this "menu" you can imagine its traditional, homely, local character. The public bar normally has some Liverpool personalities to liven up the atmosphere, and it is an alehouse where the politics of football, that most divisive of Liverpool pastimes, are discussed at some length.

The White House is not at all a spectacular pub, but then it serves a section of the local community well enough. Why it is called the White House is unknown, though photographs of U.S. presidents around the public bar suggest some significant association.

The Winslow Hotel
Everton

Opening times: Monday – Saturday, 11am – 11pm & Sunday hours.
Ales include: Tetley Bitter
Bar Snacks/Meals: No
Live Music: No
Jukebox: Yes
Fruit Machines: Yes
Function Room: No

The Winslow Hotel stands in the shadow of Goodison Park, home to Everton Football Club. It is famous for its proximity to a ground that over the years, despite being overshadowed by its close rival, has witnessed some great moments in football history. Who can forget the European nights of the mid-eighties, when Everton led the way for British clubs? The Winslow has always been a pub closely associated with the exploits of this famous football club, and it is an alehouse that benefits greatly from this proximity.

The pub, like all of the houses surrounding, is built in the old red-brick fashionable earlier in the century. It stands smartly by the junction of Winslow Street, amid the urban sprawl of Everton and like so many pubs in Liverpool is a focus for the surrounding community. The building it occupies has three storeys, with the pub on the ground floor, thus allowing for the occupation of the upper floors.

Inside, the alehouse is split into two distinctive areas. To the right of the doorway is a large split-level room, and here one can find a pool table. This half of the pub is open constantly. The room to the left of the door is only used at busy times, like on match days when the sheer number of people wanting a pre-match drink requires its use. Predictably, the décor is dominated by pictures and artifacts associated with Everton Football Club, and its various achievements over the years. The decor is quite standard, giving the pub a smart, though undistinguished, appearance.

The Winslow is a relaxed and welcoming pub that is aware of its role as a community pub, while functioning as a watering hole for supporters before football matches. It is held in high regard by most Everton fans who have had some cause to celebrate in here over the years.

Ye Cracke

13, Rice Street

Opening times: Monday – Saturday, 11.30am – 11pm & Sunday hours.
Ales include: Marston's Pedigree, Oak Best Bitter, Old Speckled Hen
Bar Snacks/Meals: Yes
Range: Extensive
Live Music: No
Jukebox: Yes
Fruit Machines: Yes
Function Room: No

Ye Cracke is a quaint, old place, standing among the narrow back streets of Liverpool in Rice Street. It is such a self-effacing place, the low whitewashed walls could be mistaken for one of the squat houses that line the rest of this tiny corner of Liverpool 1. A few old pub signs are all that signify the nature of the business conducted inside. It is a rather whimsical alehouse, lost in a past time amid the tangle of the surrounding rooftops and chimney-pots.

The pub was originally called the Ruthin Castle, and was only later nicknamed Ye Cracke. It has had an interesting history, not least for its associations with various members of the Beatles. It is remembered as an infamous drinking den of the students from the Liverpool Art College, at which prestigious establishment both Stuart Sutcliffe and John Lennon studied and socialised. Sutcliffe, who lived nearby, could often be seen drinking in Ye Cracke with his tutor and mentor, Arthur Ballard, who regarded Sutcliffe as a "brilliant student". Lennon and Sutcliffe would have boozy lunchtime sessions in here, downing black velvets with various art college associates before returning to their classes, pie-eyed and mouthy.

These days Ye Cracke has been extended so that it is not quite the elbow-to- elbow experience it was back then. The War Office still exists, a small snug towards the rear where, during the troubled times of the Boer War, men would gather to discuss the course of the war. The interior decoration consists of a haphazard collection of chairs and pews and the like, which in combination instil a great deal of charm in to this small haven.

Ye Cracke is a warm and friendly pub, one of the better pubs close to the centre. It rarely fails to appeal to newcomers – an alehouse that one will never forget.

Some other suggestions . . .

Around Liverpool 8, there are some notable houses that are worthy of a mention. The **Blackburne Arms** on the corner of Catharine Street and Falkner Street occupies a beautiful building. It is perhaps one of the most impressive cornerhouses in Liverpool, wonderfully fashioned in the Georgian style. It is well-kept and these days it remains a pleasant venue for a drink.

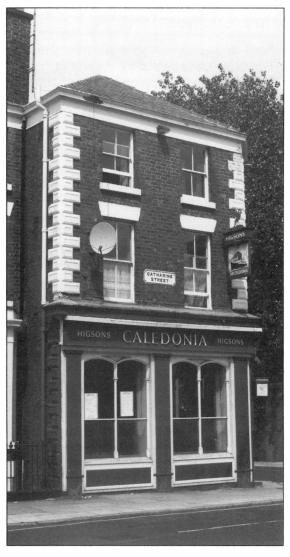

The **Caledonia**, a few yards down Catharine Street, is another corner-house – not quite as impressive as the Blackburne Arms, but equally agreeable. It is named after the famous liner which is depicted on the sign above the door.

The **Cambridge Hotel** by Mulberry Street is a most appealing place. Its smart, blue exterior enhances this corner of Liverpool. It is well-known for attracting a large student crowd, who can be seen outside on term-time evenings. It is a popular place on Sunday afternoons.

Two other notable old places are The **Lord Warden** and the **Post Office**, both in Liverpool 3. It is a refreshing point to note that the fronts of pubs like these, built in the old style, have been preserved. They look just as they did years ago, when Higsons owned most of the good houses around the city.

Finally, The **Angel** off Stanhope Street, near Sefton Street, is another house to note simply for the wonderful moulded frieze that encircles the building. In a quiet side street, the Angel has been well looked after, so that these days it is a lovely, homely old place.

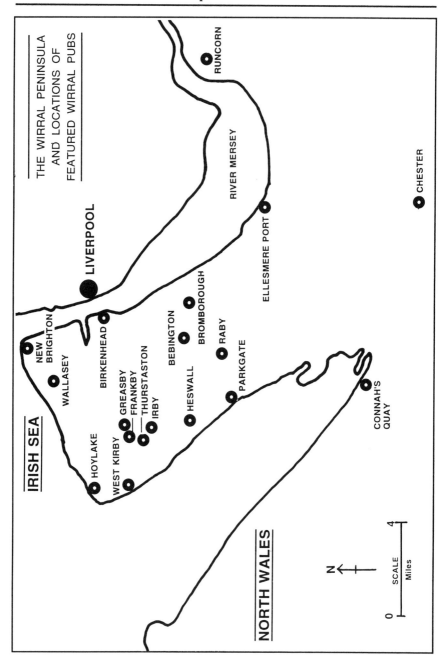

THE WIRRAL PENINSULA AND LOCATIONS OF FEATURED WIRRAL PUBS

IRISH SEA

NORTH WALES

LIVERPOOL

RIVER MERSEY

RUNCORN

CHESTER

ELLESMERE PORT

BROMBOROUGH

BEBINGTON

RABY

PARKGATE

HESWALL

CONNAH'S QUAY

NEW BRIGHTON

WALLASEY

BIRKENHEAD

GREASBY

FRANKBY

THURSTASTON

IRBY

HOYLAKE

WEST KIRBY

N

SCALE
Miles

0   4

Wirral Pubs

The Anchor Inn

Thurstaston Road, Irby.

Opening times: Monday – Saturday, 11am – 11pm & Sunday hours.

Ales include: Boddingtons, Castle Eden, Flowers, Whitbread Trophy and Mild and a guest beer.

Bar Snacks/Meals: Yes

Range: Extensive

Live Music: No

Jukebox: No (taped music)

Fruit Machines: Yes

Function Room: No

The Anchor Inn is a delightful, sandstone alehouse that in recent years has been extended. The gardens to the rear of the pub have been reduced in size over the years to adapt to the extensions. However, they are still very popular with patrons, usually young families, and offer a relaxing and peaceful place in which to enjoy a drink in the summer months.

The interior is also much changed in recent times but is perhaps a good example of an establishment that has been tastefully refurbished, without any detrimental effects on either the atmosphere or the clientele. It has been decorated in Victorian fashion, with an attractive, almost cluttered feel to the ornamentation. There is a good deal of brass-work in evidence, and nice touches are the hat-stands placed in different areas around the bar. The pub is divided into different cubby-holes so that one can normally find a place offering a little privacy. There is also a separate dining area.

Despite the fact that this part of Irby is quite built up nowadays, the Anchor Inn has the look of a smart country pub, partly to do with the smart exterior, and partly because of the gardens. A children's play area has been created here, which detracts slightly from the natural surroundings, but means that the pub is very popular with families. The Anchor is a good example of a pub that has undergone thoughtful renovation.

The Boathouse

The Parade, Parkgate

Opening times: Monday – Saturday, 11.30am – 11pm & Sunday hours.
Ales include: Greenalls Bitter, Mild and Original, Tetley.
Bar Snacks/Meals: Yes
Range: Extensive
Live Music: Yes (Sunday & Tuesday).
Jukebox: No
Fruit Machines: Yes
Function Room: Yes

The Boathouse at the beginning of the Parade in Parkgate is a delightful pub in a beautiful locality, with views of the Dee estuary. It is divided into two parts, with quite a large restaurant occupying half of the building, and an interesting and extensive bar area in the other.

The Boathouse became a pub as late as 1918. Before that, even in the last century it was a cafe, and then it was converted into a restaurant. Several different restaurants then went on to occupy the site, and this is why such a large part of the pub is given over to the restaurant area these days.

A novel feature of this pub is that it is built in the shape of a boat. Inside, the bar area has many attractive features. First, the decor is tasteful and creates a warm atmosphere in the pub without being too gaudy. There is a raised area along the river side of the pub, almost a balcony, where one may sit at a table and survey the Dee estuary. The large windows allow excellent views of the landscape. At the rear of the pub, where the bar area meets the restaurant, there is a raised extension, almost a conservatory, where one can enjoy a meal amid the beauty of the scenery; a splendid place to dine. The interior is well decorated in a traditional fashion, but without the obvious signs of refurbishment that some other pubs suffer from.

The Boathouse is a superb pub in an idyllic setting. It is well maintained throughout – including the exterior which, with a half-timbered effect and large flowering baskets, is an impressive sight. There is ample parking in front of the pub and along the parade. Parkgate itself is a very pleasant place – it used to be an up- market holiday resort until the Dee estuary silted up. Here, one can visit the Boathouse and enjoy a day along the riverside.

The Coach and Horses Inn

Greasby Road, Greasby

Opening times: Monday – Saturday, 11am – 11pm & Sunday hours.

Ales include: Whitbread Trophy and Mild

Bar Snacks/Meals: Yes

Range: Limited

Live Music: No

Jukebox: No

Fruit Machines: No

Function Room: No

The Coach and Horses is a lovely old inn that dates from the 1840s, since it is referred to in a directory of the area at this time, with one William Wilkinson as the landlord. It retains some of its original features, and these days is a delightful setting for a drink.

It is situated on the corner of Greasby Road and Mill Lane, just over the brow of the hill by the old village cross-roads. It was not the first inn in Greasby; there was an alehouse in the village in Elizabethan times. Like most alehouses then, the building was a farmhouse, and the farmer brewed and sold his own ale. The barrels of ale used to stand in a back yard, the ale being drawn up by hand pumps. In the summertime, these barrels were cooled with wet sacks.

The interior of the Coach and Horses was renovated about twenty years ago, but the walls and a few of the internal fittings of the original farm building remain. On entering, there is a small parlour to the right with a fireplace and a bench along one wall. The bar is straight ahead and is very small, with room for only a few locals to lean against. There is another snug-like room to the left of the bar decorated similarly to the first. There is also a small corner by the bar with a table and a few chairs that was known as the "rat-pit" in days past.

A print on the wall features a story from the "Liverpool Courier and Commercial Advertiser" of Wednesday 8 January,

1845. It describes how a gang of Irishmen, hired hands on a local farm, entered the pub brandishing pokers and other such weapons, with the intent to "kill all Englishmen". In the ensuing riot, the inn was wrecked, with a number of the said Englishmen crashing through the windows.

The Coach and Horses is a delightful little inn that attracts a strong local crowd, making the bar feel full on most evenings. However, it is not unwelcoming, and on summer evenings you can sit outside to savour this very old part of the village.

The Cottage Loaf

Telegraph Road, Thurstaston.

Opening times: Monday – Saturday, 11am – 11pm & Sunday hours.

Ales include: Boddingtons, Cains, Castle Eden, Speckled Hen and Whitbread Tetley.

Bar Snacks/Meals: Yes

Range: Extensive

Live Music: No

Jukebox: Yes

Fruit Machines: Yes

Function Room: No

The Cottage Loaf in Thurstaston stands alone amid the beautiful countryside of this area. It is a large pub, with ample parking space, and is quite popular with walkers and ramblers, given that it is near to Thurstaston Common. It is a convenient place to stop and rest for a while during a country walk, so it attracts a good deal of custom from day trippers.

The Cottage Loaf opened as a pub only about seven years ago, which is quite recent compared with other pubs in this guide. However, the building it occupies has been around for a considerably longer time. At the beginning of the century, tea rooms stood on this site, and an old photograph above the fireplace in the bar shows how they looked back then. As times changed, so did fashions, and the tea rooms gave way to an Italian restaurant some twenty or so years ago. The restaurant lasted for over ten years, before the buildings were bought and converted into a country pub. Nowadays, the Cottage Loaf is a pleasant pub, and at the front there is a garden with tables. It has been modernised throughout and appears to rely quite heavily on its lunchtime trade, considering that much of the bar is given over to a restaurant area.

The interior of the pub is very clean and smart with a false beamed ceiling. There is a mirrored wall on one side that combined with the rest of the décor, has the imposing feel of refurbishment. However, it does attract a good number of people probably due to its locality. If you should ever visit the Cottage Loaf, be sure to go to Thurstaston Hill and stand by the triangulation pillar and appreciate the commanding view of the land from there. It can be reached by turning right from the door of the Cottage Loaf and walking down to a car park on the right-hand side of the road. You can see the mouth of the Dee, where it empties into the Irish sea and, on a clear day, the North Wales coast.

The Crown Hotel

128, Conway Street, Birkenhead

Opening times: Monday – Saturday, 11am – 11pm & Sunday hours
Ales include: Higsons
Bar Snacks/Meals: Yes
Range: Average
Live Music: Yes
Jukebox: Yes
Fruit Machines: Yes
Function Room: Yes

The Crown is a decent alehouse in all the best senses of the words. It stands on the corner of Conway Street and Camden Place, a stout construction recently refreshed with white-washed walls and retouched flagging. It was established in 1898, and as it approaches its centenary year, it is probably one of the better-known alehouses in the centre of Birkenhead.

The combination of clean, white walls and smart burgundy ceramic makes for an attractive exterior. A huge banner draped over the doorway announces the enticement of 'Home Cooked Food', although this old world sense of well-being is tempered by the satellite dish attached to the side wall!

Inside, the narrow bar probably hasn't changed very much over the years. The back of the bar is entirely mirrored, and the sight of coloured spirit bottles stood against a glazed and etched backdrop speaks of this alehouse's age and authenticity. The pub isn't very large, although one would think from the exterior that it must be quite cavernous. The bar area is small, although there is a section to one side that holds a few tables and chairs, and some comfortable wall benches.

The atmosphere is perhaps the most attractive feature of this house. In the evenings, it is the spirited, good-natured alehouse that one would do well to find in other towns and cities, while the daytime atmosphere is more sedate. At these times, a few people normally stand up against the bar, idling away a couple of hours with friendly conversation. The clientele has a strong local element, although this brand of loyalty should not be mistaken for the icy reception one can get in some bars.

The Crown Hotel is an agreeable place that, though not particularly distinguished in any way, offers decent beer at a fair price in a time when such things are something of a rarity.

Farmers Arms
Hillbark Road, Frankby

Opening times: Monday – Saturday, 11am – 11pm & Sunday hours

Ales include: Cains Bitter, Flowers IPA, Marston's Pedigree, Whitbread Trophy and guest beers

Bar Snacks/Meals: Yes

Range: Average

Live Music: Yes (Wednesday and some Sundays)

Jukebox: No

Fruit Machines: Yes

Function Room: No

The Farmers Arms in Frankby is a delightful country inn that was opened in the October of 1866, although at that time it had no name. It was built on a piece of land purchased by the Birkenhead Amalgamated Brewery Company, close to the junction of three country lanes that afforded some, though not much, passing custom. The pub has been extended more recently, and many of the original outhouses no longer exist, but these days the Farmers Arms is still an outstanding alehouse in an idyllic setting.

The first tenant innkeeper and licensee in 1866 was Thomas Hughes, a middle-aged farmer. He kept an orderly house for six years, until 1872 when he left with his family and returned to farming. In those days, managing an alehouse was an arduous affair. The floors were covered with sawdust and required regular sweeping, fireplaces had to be cleaned and lit, and of course glasses had to be washed by hand. There were little restrictions on the sale of alcoholic beverages in those times, so that Mr Hughes opened up at around six o'clock in the morning to serve customers of any age. To add to Mr Hughes' workload, it was not as if the tenanting of a country alehouse could provide one with a living. He still had to cultivate vegetable plots for his family's requirements, to make ends meet.

These days, thankfully, the task is not quite so demanding. Despite the many changes, the pub is still a lovely place to enjoy a drink. The spacious interior is decorated in a traditional fashion, with the various artifacts associated with a rural existence on display around the bar. The gardens to the rear are quite extensive, and the addition of a children's play area attracts many young families, especially during the warmer months.

The Farmers Arms is a most agreeable alehouse with an authentic sense of history about it – one of the few original 'country' inns that still stands in unspoilt surroundings and long may it do so.

The Fox and Hounds

Barnston Road, Heswall

Opening times: Monday – Thursday, 11.30am – 3pm & 5.30pm – 11pm; Friday & Saturday, 11am – 11pm; Sunday 12pm – 3pm; 7pm – 10.30pm

Ales include: Courage Directors, Marstons Pedigree, Ruddles County Best Bitter and Mild, Websters.

Bar Snacks/Meals: Yes

Range: Average

Live Music: No

Jukebox: No

Fruit Machines: No

Function Room: No

Be careful not to miss the Fox and Hounds on Barnston Road. It stands just round a bend on the easy slope of a hill, and can be passed without noticing if one is travelling too quickly. It is a very old alehouse, probably established in or around 1754 as a coaching inn on the route between the Wirral and Chester.

The pub is set in a leafy glade, and it has a large car park to the side. The exterior looks quite authentic, particularly the pub sign hanging above the road which seems to have done so for many years. Entrance can be gained from around the back, where there are two entrances for different parts of the pub. The first entrance leads into a large room, part of which used to operate as a tea room. Just through this doorway is a wooden sign, the "table of licensees", displaying the names of different people who over the years have held the license to the Fox and Hounds. Through the second doorway, you enter the main part of the pub, where there is a smallish bar area with a snug room attached. The bar on this side has many shelves displaying a vast array of spirits, particularly whiskeys. The snug room is a fine old room. In here, green leather benches line the walls, and there is an old fireplace with a grand clock above it. An old gaming machine is attached to the wall. There is a peculiar feel to this room, almost as if it has remained unchanged over the years.

There is talk of the pub being haunted by an old lady who sits in a rocking chair. Whether this is true or not, the Fox and Hounds is a venerable old place. It is certainly another of the Wirral's notable alehouses that should appeal to those who like their pubs to have a real feeling of tradition about them.

The Greave Dunning

Greasby Road, Greasby.

Opening times: Monday – Saturday, 11am – 11pm & Sunday hours.

Ales include: Bass, Cains and Worthingtons.

Bar Snacks/Meals: Yes

Range: Extensive

Live Music: Yes (Tuesday)

Jukebox: Yes

Fruit Machines: Yes

Function Room: Yes (Free)

The Greave Dunning is a relatively young pub, especially compared with the other pubs in Greasby village. It was opened in 1983, following the conversion of derelict farm buildings, and is now the most popular alehouse in Greasby.

The interior of the pub is very large, with many different areas each with their own separate characters and clientele. The rooms to the left of the main entrance were originally the farmhouse. The main bar area through the door was once a milking parlour, while the area to the right used to be a barn. The whole pub is decorated in a traditional style, with beamed ceilings in evidence throughout. The rooms to the right are as a rule the haunt of young people, and on this side there is a large screen television fixed to the wall. The two rooms to the left include a family area, and both are divided by partitions producing lots of smaller, more private areas to drink in. It is generally quieter and more relaxed on this side of the pub.

An attractive feature of the Greave Dunning is the high balcony stretching across two of the large rooms. There are several tables up here, accommodating more people in this already large pub. Throughout the house, a pride is shown in the history of the buildings and local history through the various maps and snippets of information displayed around the walls. The Dunning of Greave Dunning refers to the name of the first overlord of Greasby. This detail is found in the Domesday Book, which is the earliest written reference to Greasby.

The Greave Dunning is a welcoming alehouse with friendly staff that is very popular and well frequented on most evenings. It is an attractive pub to look upon, with sandstone walls and hanging baskets all around the exterior. It stands near the top of the hill, by the old crossroads in what is probably the oldest part of Greasby village.

The Harvest Mouse

164, Pensby Road, Heswall.

Opening times: Monday – Saturday, 11am – 11pm & Sunday hours.

Ales include: Cains Bitter, Greenalls Bitter, Original and Mild.

Bar Snacks/Meals: Yes

Range: Extensive

Live Music: No

Jukebox: Yes

Fruit Machine: Yes

Function Room: No

The Harvest Mouse in Heswall is immediately striking because it sports a full-size windmill at the front of the pub, built and finished in the traditional style. Don't believe your eyes! Appearances are deceptive and the windmill is simply a gimmick that was built with the rest of the pub about ten years ago. With a little more thought, it is soon apparent that the positioning of the windmill would have been highly inappropriate if, as a real mill, it was hoped to catch the breeze.

The Harvest Mouse is a pub/restaurant, a phenomenon on the increase these days that reduces the character and individuality of establishments under the same company. However, the Harvest Mouse deserves some attention considering that the interior is really quite well-decorated, and that the pub has a genial atmosphere at most times of the day.

The pub is bigger than average, and consequently the open-plan design produces quite a cavernous interior. It is amply decorated, and has a huge bar area extending round most of the interior. A particularly attractive feature of the Harvest Mouse is the balcony up to the right of the bar where one can sit enabling a clear inspection of the beamed ceiling. The fittings nearer to ground level are rather standard for this type of pub, but the pub is smart and attractive. It is popular at lunchtimes, offering an extensive menu. At other times it can look a little empty because of the vastness of the interior.

The Irby Mill

Mill Lane, Greasby

Opening times: Monday – Saturday, 11.30am – 3pm; 5pm – 11pm; Sunday 7pm – 10.30pm.

Ales include: Cains Bitter and Mild, Boddingtons, Jennings and guest beers

Bar Snacks/Meals: Yes

Range: Extensive

Live Music: No

Jukebox: No

Fruit Machines: No

Function Room: No

The Irby Mill is a marvellous country pub, a real delight that satisfies the needs of its devoted customers by being a simple, honest, decent alehouse. It is situated by the junction of Mill Lane and Arrowebrook Lane, occupying a lovely sandstone building that complements the beauty of the surrounding rural corner.

The Irby Mill was opened in 1980 after the conversion of a tumbledown miller's cottage. The original windmill that stood on this site was built in the early part of the eighteenth century, and was the longest surviving mill of its type on the Wirral. The first miller, in 1725, was William Harrison of Greasby. The mill was eventually demolished in 1898 after it had been left to reach a very ruinous condition, and had become a source of danger. According to local legend, the three men who offered to pull it down did so by removing bricks from the base. The mill gave an ominous creak, before crashing down. The miller, who was watching the operation, described the workmen's escape as marvellous.

The sandstone mill cottage is difficult to date, but it is likely to have been built at the same time as the mill. It was bought by George and Bertha Lumsden in 1919 and became "The Old Mill Café" in 1924. Higsons bought the cottage in 1938 with the intention to build a country hotel, but it was only years later that they decided to convert it into a country inn. Work began in 1979, and the pub was opened in 1980.

Today, the 'Mill' is a very genial alehouse that is renowned for the quality of most of its ales. It is a small, homely place that once enjoyed is never forgotten. It is perhaps best appreciated on cold, dark nights in November or December, when the chill of the wintry air is banished, and the warmth of good company is most aptly savoured.

The Letters Inn

25 Argyle Street, Birkenhead

Opening times: Monday – Saturday, 11am – 11pm & Sunday hours.
Ales include: Cains, Chesters
Bar Snacks/Meals: Yes
Range: Extensive
Live Music: No
Jukebox: Yes
Fruit Machines: Yes
Function Room: Yes

The Letters Inn stands on Argyle Street, near the corner of the western side of Hamilton Square. It is situated right in the heart of the business section of Birkenhead: Hamilton Square is well-known for the number of professionals that do business in its Victorian buildings. The Letters occupies the ground floor of a four- storeyed affair built in similar fashion. The front is plain, but elegant, with etched windows creating the impression of some homely last century alehouse.

Inside, the pub is quite modern: decorated in a standard fashion but agreeable nonetheless. The bar is U-shaped, and is the first thing one encounters on entering the pub. There are separate areas, the one to the right of the door has a television. To the left is a large area that is usually closed in the evening, which in the daytime is used as a dining area and is usually bustling with office workers. There is also a smaller area on the back wall behind the bar that seats about ten people offering a little more privacy.

The Letters was a common name for alehouses in the last century, and was usually given to pubs that had no real title under which to trade. Alehouses were commonly named after their respective landlords, so that an alehouse that was not named so was referred to simply as 'The Letters'.

All in all, the Letters is a welcoming pub, with friendly staff that produce one of the pleasantest atmospheres of any pub in the centre of Birkenhead. It is a popular house, and on weekend evenings it can get very busy. The jukebox is loud, but has a good selection of music, and contributes to the general rumble of good-naturedness.

The Red Lion

The Parade, Parkgate

Opening times: Monday – Saturday, 12pm – 11pm & Sunday hours.

Ales include: Walker's Bitter, Best Bitter and Mild and a guest beer.

Bar Snacks/Meals: Yes

Range: Limited

Live Music: No

Jukebox: Yes

Fruit Machine: Yes

Function Room: No

The Red Lion occupies a prime position along the Parade in Parkgate. It is centrally placed, and has perfect views of the River Dee and the North Wales coastline, both of which can be enjoyed if one sits along the riverside on a summer's evening. It is close to the famous Nicholl's Ice-cream shop and it similarly attracts a good deal of custom from day trippers and tourists.

The Red Lion is set back slightly from the main street, behind the other shop fronts. It is an impressive building that complements the front along this Victorian holiday resort. The outside is well-kept, as are most of the buildings around it, which like the Red Lion have half-timbered fronts.

Inside the pub, there are two areas, one on either side of the entrance. The rooms to the right have the distinctive feel of a locals' bar, while the rooms to the left of the door are perhaps more of a public bar. Both are decorated in a manner befitting an alehouse of this stature and location, and the interior has a comfortable and almost homely feel.

The area to the left is lavishly decorated, and features a number of posters offering rewards for information about smugglers and other such ancient scoundrels. "Wanted for Smuggling; Reward five hundred pounds" announces one by the bar. Other associations with Parkgate's past are the paintings and pictures depicting many different ships that may have passed Parkgate before the Dee estuary silted up preventing their passage.

The Red Lion is a lovely pub that benefits greatly from its beautiful locality. With the other attractions in Parkgate, one can spend a most pleasant day here.

Ring O'Bells

Village Road, West Kirby

Opening times: Monday – Saturday, 11am – 11pm & Sunday hours

Ales include: Boddingtons, Whitbread Trophy and a variety of guest beers

Bar Snacks/Meals: Yes

Range: Extensive

Live Music: Yes (Thursday)

Jukebox: Yes

Fruit Machines: Yes

Function Room: No

This is an attractive pub, close to West Kirby centre, but set in a narrow, twisting lane heading towards Old Caldy. Standing in this rural corner, it looks like one of those fine, old coaching inns that were common in this remarkable peninsula. There may have been just such an inn on this site. Nowadays, the Ring O'Bells is a pleasant pub enjoyed by locals, and by people willing to travel to appreciate the unique atmosphere.

The Ring O'Bells has been recently refurbished so that while it has the excessively ordered appearance of a restaurant/pub type establishment, it is well furnished with some pleasant drinking areas. Inside, through the porch, the first area is well laid out with bookshelves lining the walls, and tables and chairs of varying size and design, each set curiously named after a different bird. The bar is split level, and one goes down a couple of steps to the main bar area. Here, and further towards the rear of the pub, there are more seats. Down by the rear of the bar is the food service area, and a large glass case tantalisingly displays the extravagant desserts on offer. The interior is well decorated without being gaudy in any way, and produces the genial atmosphere of rural contentment.

Outside, the half-timbered exterior complements the beauty of the area. In front of the pub there is a large car-park, with a paddock to the side. Here, picnic tables allow one to sit outside on warmer evenings, and during the summer this pursuit is very popular. A children's play area has been added, drawing the much-desired custom of young families to the pub in the summertime.

The Shrewsbury Arms

38, Claughton Firs, Birkenhead

Opening times: Monday – Saturday, 11am – 11pm & Sunday hours.

Ales include: Cains

Bar Snacks/Meals: Yes

Range: Extensive

Live Music: No

Jukebox: Yes

Fruit Machines: Yes

Function Room: No

The Shrewsbury Arms is a lovely alehouse, situated amid the tidy back streets of the south of Birkenhead. There is a large beer garden in front of the pub, one of its many attractive features, also a large car-park across the road. The smart exterior of whitewashed walls with black fittings sits well among the greenery of this very pleasant corner.

Inside, the pub is open-plan with a large door to the right. There are French windows in a little area to the left that open onto the beer garden. It is the garden in front of the pub that is probably the most appealing characteristic of this pub. It is hardly a garden though, more of a patio really, since it is mostly paved. Raised areas are used as seats, and in the evening, especially summer weekend evenings, the area swarms with people, creating a unique ambience. There is something very special about the 'Shrew' that is hard to describe. The large trees growing in the patio produce a very pleasant shaded effect, and when darkness falls, the lamps concealed in their branches illuminate the ground below. Even on cold winter nights, people huddle round with a glass of some warming brew in hand.

It is perhaps more popular with young people, although drinkers of all ages can be found here. People have been known to travel from as far away as Chester to enjoy its own special atmosphere. The Shrew is a delightful place where one can normally enjoy good company in a lively setting. It is best appreciated on warm early summer evenings, when many people congregate outside and when the pleasing hum of conversation can be heard around the streets.

The Wheatsheaf
Raby

Opening times: Vary

Ales include: Burton Ale, Courage Directors, Jennings, Old Peculiar, Tetley, Theakstons XB, Thwaites Traditional and Youngers.

Bar Snacks/Meals: Yes

Range: Extensive

Live Music: No

Jukebox: No

Fruit Machines: No

Function Room: No

The Wheatsheaf in Raby may be quite difficult to find, but it is certainly worth the effort. It is a delightful country inn that occupies an original seventeenth century half-timbered cottage with a thatched roof. Apparently, there has been an inn here since 1611, and though the building has been extended, with extra rooms added later, it is a wonderful, authentic setting for a drink.

The Wheatsheaf stands in an idyllic setting on a small country lane, opposite a paddock attached to a farmhouse. During the summer months, tables and chairs are available in front of the pub, so that patrons can enjoy the scenery. Inside, the authenticity continues with an original stone-flagged floor, and with dark-stained beamed ceilings throughout. The atmosphere is one of affluent, country living, but these days it attracts as many people willing to search for its scenic beauty, as it does local country dwellers.

The pub is split into three areas: a main bar area with rooms to the left and right. the decoration is tasteful, and in keeping with the general feeling of rural life. The room to the left is small enough to be a snug, while the room to the right is a delightful place for a drink, with low lighting producing a most agreeable ambience.

The Wheatsheaf is a lovely old alehouse. Finding it for the

first time, one marvels at the sight of its features, as one turns into the small lane leading to its front. Hanging baskets decorate the exterior as if any more decoration was needed. The Wheatsheaf has many interesting features, not least the extensive range of real ales on offer, and is recommended to anyone with a car and the wish to escape the dusty city.

Some other suggestions . . .

In and around the centre of Birkenhead, there are many alehouses that are noted here for their fine construction.

The **Royal Castle** on the road to Tranmere is an impressive sight. This huge brick building is really quite remarkable not least for its strange location. It is constructed on such a large scale that it dominates its surrounds, with wonderful prominences of all descriptions, and an unusual balcony on one corner.

The **Meadows Hotel** is another splendid 'vault'. The exterior of this grand, old place is beautifully proportioned, with good use of ceramic around the ground floor level. It is a well-known alehouse within Birkenhead, and so attracts a varied crowd at most times.

Other pubs around the Wirral deserve a mention, including the **Dee Hotel** in the centre of West Kirby. Here is a vast, half-timbered alehouse set back from the road. A truly imposing place!

The **Arrowe Park Hotel** is another stately place. It stands by the back entrance to Arrowe Park, on a busy roundabout. It has recently been refurbished, and offers the drinker a delightful atmosphere.

Index

This index lists the names of all establishments listed in the book, with cross references to any other names by which they have been known. Streets are included to assist in locating pubs in a particular locality. Names of the main breweries or their products are in **bold type**.

A

Albert Dock	67
Albert, The	65
Anchor Inn, The	90
Anfield	65, 78
Angel, The	87
Arrowe Park Hotel, The	115

B

Baltic Fleet, The	67
Bass	21, 37, 43, 47, 51, 53, 61, 63, 65, 102
Beatles, The	29
Beehive, The	8
Birkenhead	98, 107, 110, 114
Blackburne Arms	85
Boathouse, The	92
Boddingtons	45, 69, 90, 96, 105, 109
Burton Ales	73, 112

C

Cains	4, 10, 22, 24, 27, 29, 45, 51, 53, 57, 61, 69, 71, 73, 96, 99, 102, 104 - 107, 110
Caledonia, The	86
Cambridge Hotel	86
Cammell Laird	34

Cases Street	14, 27
Castle Eden	75, 90, 96
Catharine Street	86
Central, The	12
Cheapside	51
Chesters	107
Coach and Horses, The	94
Coopers	14
Cornmarket Hotel	16
Cottage Loaf, The	96
Courage Directors	16, 31, 101, 112
Covent Garden	39
Crown Hotel, The	98
Crown, The	18
Cumberland Street	41

D

Dale Street	41, 49, 51, 53, 63
Dee Hotel, The	115
Derby Square	43
Dr Duncan's	20
Duke Street	80

E

Eagle, The	21
Empire, The	22

More books from Sigma Leisure

We publish a wide range of books for North-West England and further afield. Here is a small selection:

Best Pub Walks in & around Manchester	£6.95
Best Pub Walks around Chester & The Dee Valley	£6.95
Best Pub Walks on Merseyside	£6.95
Pub Walks in Lancashire	£6.95
Pub Walks in the Lake District	£6.95
Seashore Sea Food: How to Catch it, Cook it and Prepare it!	£4.95
Traditional Pubs of Old Lancashire	£7.95
Golf Courses of Cheshire	£9.95
50 Best Cycle Rides in Cheshire	£7.95
Cycling in The Lake District	£7.95
100 Lake District Hill Walks	£7.95
Lakeland Walking: On The Level	£6.95
Teashop Walks in The Lake District	£6.95
Lakeland Rocky Rambles: geology beneath your feet	£9.95
Mostly Downhill (series of 3 books covering the Lake District, Dark Peak and White Peak)	£6.95 each
Rambles around Manchester	£5.95
Ghosts, Traditions amd Legends of Old Lancashire	£7.95
Portrait of Manchester	£6.95
Great Days Out! Manchester area	£4.95

All of our books are available from your bookseller. In case of difficulty, or for our complete catalogue, please contact:

Sigma Leisure, 1 South Oak Lane, Wilmslow, Cheshire SK9 6AR. Tel: 01625-531035; Fax: 01625-536800

Cheques payable to SIGMA PRESS.
Major credit cards welcome